Steaming to Bamboola

Steaming to Bamboola

THE WORLD OF A
TRAMP FREIGHTER

Christopher Buckley

Essex, Connecticut

An imprint of Globe Pequot, the trade division of
The Rowman & Littlefield Publishing Group, Inc.
4501 Forbes Blvd., Ste. 200
Lanham, MD 20706
www.rowman.com

Distributed by NATIONAL BOOK NETWORK

Many quotes and most of the information in "Mrs. Wilson's Burden" have
been taken from Don H. Kennedy, *Ship Names: Origins and Usages During 45
Centuries* (Charlottesville: University of Virginia Press, 1974).

The historical material on the old Snug Harbor in "Snug Harbor" is from Barnett
Shepard, *Sailors' Snug Harbor: 1801 to 1976* (New York: Snug Harbor, 1979).

British Library Cataloguing in Publication Information available

Library of Congress Cataloging-in-Publication Data

The Congdon & Lattès edition of this book was previously catalogued by the
Library of Congress as follows:

Buckley, Christopher Taylor.
Steaming to Bamboola.

1. Columbianna (Steamship) 2. Ocean travel.
I. Title.
G540.B79   1982   910.4'1   81-17291

ISBN 9781493073924 (paper : alk. paper) | ISBN 9781493076635 (ebook)

∞™ The paper used in this publication meets the minimum requirements of
American National Standard for Information Sciences — Permanence of Paper for
Printed Library Materials, ANSI/NISO Z39.48-1992.

Author's Note

The ship, the people, and the events are real.
The names of the ship and her crew were changed.

In memory of
John Lennon
1940–1980,
son of a merchant seaman

Contents

A gone shipmate, like any other man, is gone forever; and I never met one of them again. But at times the spring-flood of memory sets with force up the dark River of the Nine Bends. Then on the waters of the forlorn stream drifts a ship—a shadowy ship manned by a crew of Shades. They pass and make a sign, in a shadowy hail. Haven't we, together and upon the immortal sea, wrung out a meaning from our sinful lives? Good-bye, brothers! You were a good crowd. As good a crowd as ever fisted with wild cries the beating canvas of a heavy foresail; or tossing aloft, invisible in the night, gave back yell for yell to a westerly gale.

Joseph Conrad
The Nigger of the "Narcissus"

Introduction

Steaming to Bamboola was my first book, and if you'll forgive the cliché, like any first-born it occupies a special place in my heart. I was in my twenties then. I'm on my eighth decade now, and 19 books later, am wondering if books are ever going to get any easier to write before I "cross the bar." If the line from Tennyson makes the reader groan, I can at least plead in my defense that I managed to write an entire maritime-themed book without quoting Masefield's "I must go down to the seas again."

Such merit as the book has is largely due to its editor, the late Thomas Congdon. Tom is slightly better known for having edited another sea story called *Jaws*. You may have heard of it. He edited everyone from Peter Benchley to Russell Baker and A. Scott Berg. Tom defined an editor as "someone who makes love to authors." Forty years later, I still pinch myself at my good fortune in having him as my first book editor.

And 40 years later, I still remember—vividly—his reaction to the manuscript I delivered: "It's wonderful. It's even better than I'd had hoped it would be."

I walked on air.

Two weeks later a 50 page, single-spaced "memo" with "suggestions" arrived in the mail. The air on which I'd been walking went *pfft*. I fell to earth like Icarus, cratering.

I phoned him, stammering, "But . . . but I thought you said it was wonderful?"

"It *is*," he purred, "and it's going to be even *more* wonderful."

His first suggestion was to cut the opening section, which I'd somewhat grandiosely titled "Book One," from 150 pages to one and a half pages. *Bamboola*'s Prologue is all that remains of my epic original "Book One."

At college, I studied under Bill Zinsser, the legendary writing teacher whose mantra was "Be grateful for every word you can cut." I can't describe my reaction to Tom's suggestion as "grateful." "Suicidal" would be more accurate. But he was right.

Now, 40 years later, I'm grateful to Rick Rinehart and Globe Pequot for reissuing *Bamboola* and in the process, providing me an excuse to reveal what was in "Book One." Doubtless, the world has been waiting with bated breath all these four decades. I'll try to do it in less than 150 pages.

After graduating from boarding school, where during winters I stood on iced-over Narragansett Bay and watched the big ships go out to sea (see Prologue), I signed aboard a Norwegian tramp freighter as a deck boy. My pay was twenty dollars a week and forty cents an hour overtime. But a case of beer from the ship's store cost three bucks, and a cartoon of cigarettes, one buck, making me wealthier at age eighteen than I've ever been since.

M.V. *Fernbrook* was a 520-foot dry cargo freighter with a crew of 33 souls: mostly Norwegians, two Danes, one German, and five Chinese. I was the only American. Not everyone spoke English, but we somehow communicated. (The beer helped.)

She took me around the world: New York, South Carolina, Panama Canal, San Pedro, San Francisco, Manila, Hong Kong, Bangkok, Singapore, Belawan, Penang, Phuket, Cochin (India), Colombo (Ceylon, as it was then called), ending with a 33-day passage back to New York via the Cape of Good Hope, enlivened by a Force 12 gale in the South Atlantic.

In 1970, container ships were just beginning to come into service, so I was among the last generation of seamen to work on cargo ships that still looked *like* ships, unlike today's, which resemble enormous Lego constructions. Back then—dare I say "in my day"?—you knew what cargoes you were carrying because you could see them, smell them, touch them, and on occasion, help yourself to them. As cast members of *The Sopranos* say by way of explaining their new 53-inch plasma screen TV, "It fell off the back of the truck."

Fernbrook's five holds were like giant grandfather attics stuffed with everything and anything. All these years later, I can still inventory her cargoes from memory: a traffic light for Singapore; generators; rolls of coiled steel; ping pong balls; ceramic mugs; cans of whipped cream; penicillin; firearms; a Volkswagon; sacks of concrete; zillions of IBM computer punch cards; cigarettes; baby food; paperback books; tinned peaches; paraffin; Parker pens; Ivory soap; lipstick; barrels of machine oil, kerosene; apples; baseball bats; TVs; radios; light bulbs; and, uh, crates of Scotch whiskey that had an odd tendency to get dropped and bust open.

While crossing the Pacific, the equatorial sun turned the steel decks into frying pans. I took my lunch hour by climbing down a 50-foot ladder into the lowermost, refrigerated hold, which in San Francisco we'd filled with mountains of loose Oregon apples. I'd jump off the ladder onto the top of the nearest apple mound, eat a half dozen—oh, they were good!—belch like a contented seal, and lie back and catch 40 winks. Those lunch hours remain my definition of worldly bliss.

On our way back from the Far East, we carried mostly raw goods: burlap sacks of cocoanut shell charcoal; sacks of loose tea; tin ingots; sisal; liquid latex; drums of coconut oil; teak; mahogany; oils and spices. We were a fragrant ship.

Assorted memories:

In Manila, ducking as bullets *tink-tink-tinked* against our hull, a cop firing a machine at two *very* fast-footed thieves, who escaped by diving into the sharky water between us and the wharf. Watching a huge crate labeled "MANILA PUBLIC SCHOOLS" slip loose of the cargo straps and crash 20 feet to the deck, nearly killing two stevedores and spilling forth hundreds of paperback *Collected Stories of Guy de Maupassant*.

In Hong Kong, waking up on New Year's Day with a paint-stripping hangover, wondering why my bicep was on fire. The tattoo is faded but still there, 52 years later.

In Bangkok, coming on deck before dawn as we motored upriver and watching the sun set fire to a half dozen gold-leafed pagodas that rose above the jungle canopy.

In Phuket, anchoring off the beach, then miles of pristine sand and not a building in sight. Barges brought our cargo of tin ingots.

In Cochin as we approached the dock, police drove back the horde of beggars to prevent them from throwing their children into our propellers, so as to maim them and make them more efficient beggars.

In Colombo, walking barefoot on crunchy sacks of cinnamon as they were lowered into the hold. Buying a star sapphire. A last drink ashore before the long voyage home.

Standing the midnight to 4 a.m. watch on the leg home, staring endlessly at the horizon in search of other ships. One night, seeing the lights of Saint Helena.

During the storm, taking 30-minute spells at the helm, intensely concentrated on keeping our bow perpendicular into the mountainous seas. On being relieved, my hands shaking too hard to light a cigarette. The roller-coaster feel as the ship crested each wave, the heart-stopping moment of weightlessness before the plunge into the trough, the shudder as she rose, slowly and whale-like from the boiling froth. Afterwards, seeing her inch-thick steel bow crumpled like a beer can and learning that two ships had gone down in the storm.

My last night on watch, seeing the great turnstile sweep of the Ambrose Light off New York, 4 months and 32,890 miles later. The log entry "FWE"—finished with engines. Voyage done.

Much compressed, that was *Bamboola's* "Book One" before Captain Congdon said, "Enough throat-clearing! Cut to the chase!"

Fernbrook stayed with me through college and the early years of a career as a journalist and editor. Having made it this far without quoting Masefield, I'll refrain from mooning about the lonely seas and the sky, other than to say that I spent a decade conniving an excuse to—oh, I give up—"go down to the seas" again.

Finally, in 1980, weirdly 10 years to the day since *Fernbrook* sailed out of New York harbor on a cold November night, I walked up the clanky gangplank of the S.S. *Columbianna* in Charleston, South Carolina. I made a half-dozen winter North Atlantic crossings aboard her. Unlike "Book One," there's no "I" in *Steaming to Bamboola* (other than in the Prologue). It's not about me. It's about a ship and her crew, real seamen, unlike the one I fancied myself to be at eighteen. This makes it a better, more worthy story.

John Lennon was murdered while I was writing the book. That cast a pall. His father having been a merchant seaman, I dedicated the book to John's memory. On the occasion of *Bamboola*'s relaunch, I rededicate it, in Joseph Conrad's splendid phrasing, to my "gone shipmates."

Prologue

When I was thirteen, I was sent off to a New England boarding school run by monks. It was not a terrible place, by English standards, though by American a bit on the grim side. There was an old Latin teacher overly fond of beating his pupils with a wet sneaker who once told a boy he should be sent to Vietnam because he did not remember what *denique* ("in a nutshell") meant. Boys found smoking were expelled and assured this would end their chances of getting into a decent college and therefore of amounting to anything in life. They were taught that virtue was knowing the meaning of *denique* and that Hell was real. It was a good school, academically, and sent a lot of graduates to Yale and Harvard.

During the Rhode Island winters when the sun set before five, it was a cheerless, isolated place that looked down onto a frozen bay. Boys were forbidden to leave the grounds, but one day I discovered a half-measure of escape by walking way out onto the ice, almost a mile from shore, right up to the edge of the channel cut by the big ships. I would stand there watching the freighters come and go. The monks finally caught me at this and henceforth made it punishable by expulsion. (They envisioned little bodies in navy blue blazers turning up with the spring thaw.) Still, I went out when I could, even if it did jeopardize my chances of amounting to anything in life.

One afternoon as I stood on the edge of the ice, an old

Victory ship steamed by, passing so close I felt the vibrations of her propeller under my feet. Her name was *Hannibal Victory*. She was loaded down and outward bound.

Leaning over the taffrail, one of her crewmen was having a smoke. It probably startled him to see a small boy in school uniform standing on the edge of the ice, hands in his pockets, a mile out from shore. The seaman's face creased into a grin. He laughed. And then with a wave of his arm he beckoned at me to jump for it. The seaman laughed again, unaware of the effect of his gesture on me. I watched him until he was only a speck on the poop deck of a ship disappearing out to sea.

The Ship

Our vessel was a beautiful ship of about four hundred tons, copper fastened, and built at Bombay of Malabar teak. She was freighted with cotton-wood and oil, from the Laccadive islands. We also had on board coir, jaggeree, ghee, cocoa-nuts, and a few cases of opium. The stowage was clumsily done and the vessel consequently crank.

Edgar Allan Poe
"A MS Found in a Bottle"

HER BED LINEN WAS WORN THIN FROM USE. THE SHEETS HAD little holes that unclipped toenails turned into gashes. A pillowcase was stamped, in fading block letters, USNS TALLULAH. There was a large bloodstain on it, an old one—from a head wound, more likely, rather than a nosebleed. It was ironic the Bed Room steward passed out bloodstained pillowcases: the Captain had nicknamed him "the Ghost" because of the way he disappeared without a noise while a person talking to him was in mid-sentence. The Ghost was a wet-eyed, prematurely graybeard Norwegian. The Nazis had strafed his village when he was twelve, flying so low he remembered the face of the pilot. He left home after the war and had spent his life at sea, mostly as a Bed Room steward. He had an ethereal disposition; in another time people would have said he was "touched." He spent hours sitting up on the bow talking, so he said, with King Neptune. The Ghost sometimes

1

talked in rhyme; made puns like "I may be low rate, but don't underrate me," and then would toodle off, mop in hand, white rags hanging from his back pockets, laughing to himself. He made the Captain nervous.

She was an old ship. Her history was written into her hull, a patchwork of dings and cicatrices from thirty-five years of banging into things on the watery hither and yon. A few months ago she'd rammed into a tender in the Suez Canal, and had sunk it. The evidence was a five-foot dent just aft of the stem on her port side. Dozens of pockmarks had been struck into her stern by crucifixes—the cleats on barges—when she carried the last load of ammo into Da Nang in January 1974. Beneath her bow badge a lot of welding had been done; it looked like healed-over scar tissue from a bad burn. In 1978, under another captain, she had plowed into a Coast Guard cutter tied up to the dock in Mobile. Mr. Dexter, her present third mate, had been aboard then. He was at his post on the bow when she hit and was thrown ten feet by the impact. He picked himself off the deck, called the captain on the walkie-talkie, and said, "What the hell goes on here?" The relief captain, an excitable Albanian, told him, "Don't tell anyone! Don't tell anyone!"

"Here we were," said Mr. Dexter, recounting the event, "our bow stuck in a United States Coast Guard cutter, maybe four ships coming in and out the harbor, probably two hundred people watching, everyone aboard knocked ass over teakettle— my back hasn't been right since—and he's telling me, 'Don't *tell* anyone!' 'Oh,' I said to myself, 'this is no good at all.' "

Her decks were covered with over two hundred layers of paint. By digging into them with a knife, a person could tell what colors had been laid on, all the way back to 1945. Great, lichenous flakes of smokestack carbon adhered to everything. The decks were cobwebbed with antennae wires that generations of crewmen had strung from the portholes up onto deck. By the time a new crewman had memorized where they all were, he had been garroted several times while walking the deck at night. Because of irreparably clogged drainpipes, there were areas in her super-

2

structure that collected rainwater and spray. When she rolled more than ten degrees, someone having a quiet smoke could get sopped with warm brackish water.

As with most ships, there was a social hierarchy that prevailed within her seven decks. The lowermost deck was for the crew quarters. Many of the focsles on this level held three or four men each. (The term *focsle*—pronounced *"folk-* sull"—is a shortening of forecastle, the old term for the communal area near the box where the entire crew, except for the officers, once lived and ate. These days *focsle* has simply come to mean "cabin." There were a number of three- and four-man focsles on the *Columbianna.* Over the years, about two thousand men had lived in each one. The focsles showed the hard use, even though they had been coated and recoated with Mint Frappe paint. The entire inside of the ship had been painted in Mint Frappe, an insincere shade of green, presumably meant to brighten the spirits of those who had to walk the catacomb of passageways and look at exposed overhead piping, warty, protruding rivets, and faded, chipped linoleum.

On the second deck were the messhalls, the washing machines, some single and double focsles, the galley, and the Slop Chest, where every Saturday afternoon the Captain sold cigarettes, soda pop, blue jeans, toothpaste, candy bars, hair tonic, and other items. The name *Slop Chest* derives from the old English *sloppe,* the ragged breeches once worn by seamen on British warships and sold to the men out of chests by the pursers.

The next deck up housed the officers' cabins, as well as the main doors to the engine room. The gaskets on those doors did little to stifle the noise generated by the steam turbines and boilers. The smell of Bunker C fuel was pervasive, but after a few days the nose adapted.

Above was the superstructure. In ascending order of decks: the ship's office and the main electrical and gyroscope rooms; the focsle of Sparks, the radio operator and his radio room; the Captain's cabin, office, and day room; and above that, the bridge and chart room. Two observation decks protruded from either side of the bridge, buttressed from beneath by steel struts. These were the wing decks, where the lookouts kept their watch, and from which, on a clear night, the horizon was almost ten miles off.

She still had her original plumbing. Each toilet was possessed by a different demon. One made an exploding sound when flushed, followed by a raucous sucking noise. Another needed seven or eight flushes before it would swallow even a cottonball. Another emitted two bangs, three seconds apart, every time it was flushed. At one time the Chief Mate's did not stop flushing for a month and two days. The men from the engine room went at it but could do nothing. Then suddenly one day, it ceased gurgling, and let the Chief Mate alone.

Running in ballast, the ship vibrated like a washing machine during the spin cycle. Her Joshua Hendy nine-thousand-horsepower steam turbines gave her a cruising speed of sixteen knots at seventy-eight revolutions per minute. Fully loaded, and with her engines put full astern, she took a half mile and three-and-a-half minutes to come to a full stop. Turning on a dime was not one of her abilities. At full speed, with the rudder hard over, the tightest circle she could make had a diameter of one mile.

When the metal door to the skipper's cabin rattled a certain way, it meant she was making cruising speed. A hum throughout the top three decks indicated the wind was blowing Force Seven or better. When the wind hit Force Eight, it spun the propellers on the lifeboats. Nine years ago, when the ship was being rebuilt, a workman left some tools and ball bearings welded in the ceiling above the captain's bunk. By now the Captain had grown accustomed to the sound of stainless steel balls rolling across ten feet of metal ceiling, bouncing off rivets and seams, followed by the scraping of a wrench (he supposed), which slid only when she rolled more than twenty-five degrees.

Her keel was laid at the Kaiser yard in Vancouver, Washington, and she was launched seven months later on July 10, 1945, with the name *S.S. Marine Bobcat*—a 12,420-gross ton, 523-foot troop ship. She was built for the invasion of Japan, but the atomic bomb, dropped on Hiroshima a month after she was shipped down the ways, vitiated her wartime purpose. Instead, *Marine Bobcat* shuttled back and forth across the Pacific, carrying troops home and fresh occupation soldiers to Japan, 2,926 men per trip. In 1945 she had a crew of 219. By 1947, she was already becoming obsolete, and was mothballed. Then war broke out in Korea. Between 1950 and 1954, she made twenty-two trips from Seattle to Korea and Japan, earning seven battle stars, one of them for taking part in MacArthur's Inchon landing. After the fall of Dien Bien Phu in 1954, she was used to evacuate refugees fleeing the Communists in the "Passage to Freedom" operation. She made six round trips from Haiphong to Saigon.

In 1958, she was mothballed again. This time she spent ten years at anchor in the Columbia River, near Astoria, Oregon, until she was sold—for the third time—to a company that had special plans for her. The new owners intended to send her back to Vietnam, but as a cargo ship.

A tug brought her from Astoria through the Panama Canal to the Newport News shipyard in Virginia. The forward bridge house was sawed off, taken way aft and welded on over the engine house. (It was presumably during this phase of the redesign that the wrench and ball bearings were added to the captain's ceiling.) The troop quarters were gutted and made into cargo holds. The brig, where unruly troops and seamen were jailed, they decided to keep. Six king posts were installed, raked outwardly so as to form three imposing Vs in a row, rising high off her deck. The king posts supported three 100-foot-long, 45-ton Stuelcken booms, rigged with over a mile of 1¼-inch steel cable. Each boom could lift 120 tons of cargo; "wedded" together, 240 tons, which gave her, at the time, the heaviest lifting capacity of any U.S. ship afloat. To prevent her from tipping over while hoisting 240 tons of cargo, two 296-ton ballast tanks were added, one on each side.

It was an expensive redesign, but the new owners were gambling that, during the Vietnam sealift, they'd get the heavy cargoes other ships couldn't handle: landing craft, locomotives, planes, artillery pieces. When the ship was finished, her dead-weight tonnage, or carrying capacity, was 11,187 tons. A bottle of champagne was slammed against her bow as she was rechristened with a euphonious, less bellicose name, the S.S. *Columbianna*.

The owners gambled well. She carried a lot of materiel to

5

Vietnam. Since 1969 she has earned $39.7 million worth of net business, sailing more or less everywhere in the small world of tramps. One fairly routine trip took her from Norfolk to Bermuda, Guantanamo, Buenos Aires, Terceira, Southampton, Glasgow, Rota, Kenitra, Piraeus, Assab, and Boston. Some of the other ports of call are listed in her logbooks: Port Said, Kompong Som, Aqaba, Bikini, Sattahip, Naha, Poro Island, Sunny Point, Keelung, Vung Tau, Subic Bay, Eniwetok, Iwakuni, Zeebrugge, Iskenderun, La Pallice, Mocha, Ashdod, Nassau, Jedda, Limon, Lisbon, Cristobal, Gravesend, Livorno, Iraklion, Hodeida, Alexandria.

She has carried all sorts of cargoes: a $100-million missile tracking system from California to Kwajalein, its fifty-four-ton antenna packed in tons of drying agent; an entire radio station from Belfast to the States; a very hot, top secret shipment of Russian T-62 tanks and 16-mm field artillery pieces captured on the Golan Heights during the Yom Kippur War; and, at various other times, ambulances, bombs, timber, steel, mobile homes, helicopters, bullets, booze, and a hitchhiking, banded carrier pigeon who joined the *Columbianna* at Torbay, England. Nicknamed Little Willy by the crew, he ate a diet of Grape-Nuts and stayed on for the transatlantic passage, disembarking at Key West.

Now the *Columbianna*'s holds were stuffed with flatbed trailers, station wagons, a Lincoln Continental, a Toyota that ended up rather more compact than it started out, six buses, submachine guns, grenades, tractors, "sensitive weapons" locked tight inside a container, two dozen M-60 tanks, thirty-six refrigerators, pumps, radar sets, and two hundred cases of bourbon whiskey. The weapons and the whiskey were for NATO.

It no longer made much difference to the Captain *what* he was carrying "across the pond." In thirty-six years of sailing he had lost count altogether of how many times he had traversed the North Atlantic. More than a hundred, he guessed: three-and-a-half years of crossings, measured consecutively. One night, on this voyage, he tried to recall the cargoes he had taken from one side

6

of the ocean to the other. Tanks, half-tracks, cannons, cork, chrome ore. Coal, coke, almonds, puncheons of wine, olives, laxatives (in bottles which the crew mistook for booze, and drank), tin ingots, phosphates, flour, passengers ("the most precious of all cargoes," he remarked, apparently remembering an unpleasant experience). The list grew longer. Wheat, corn, soldiers, gasoline, oranges, DPs (displaced persons: "the most semiprecious of all cargoes"—he had to bury a lot of them at sea), crude, JP-4, JP-5, televisions, radios, lathes, locomotives, airplanes, operating tables, penicillin, sulfa, scalpels, money, postwar PX scrip welded into a forward compartment, typewriters, cameras, jute, cotton, baled rubber, beef sides, potatoes, houses, pine, white ash, maple, sulphur, lampblack, manganese ore, beer, gin, frozen fish, missiles. ". . . One most perilous and long voyage ended," wrote Melville, "only begins a second; and a second ended, only begins a third, and so on, for ever and for aye. Such is the endlessness, yea, the intolerableness of all earthly effort." The quote, read to the Captain, gave him pause. "Kind of a rut, ain't it?" he said.

The king posts, those three Vs rising off the *Columbianna*'s foredeck, gave her an unusual appearance; unique, actually: no other ship had as many of them. The crew had a simile, said she looked like a dead cockroach on its back with its legs up in the air. Coming up the Mississippi one dawn, a river pilot said she looked like something much worse. The Captain's children, when they were little, called her The Ship with Grasshopper Legs, and could always tell if their father's ship was in by looking at the harbor, even from a distance. Her beauty depended greatly on who beheld it. Still, she had a battered, queenly aspect missing in the new streamlined containerships, supertankers, and certainly the Liquefied Natural Gas (LNG) carriers. Surrounded by Portuguese men-of-war when she broke down and floated in midocean, or coming up the Mississippi out of a fog bank, or nudged by Dutch tugs into a lock, she looked like what she was, an old tramp steamer, ready, as one of the crew said, to take on any port in the world, but living on borrowed time.

From Here to Bamboola

AT FIVE IN THE MORNING, TWO DAYS BEFORE THANKSGIVING, 1979, the *Columbianna*'s lines were slipped off the bits of a dock a few miles upriver from Charleston, South Carolina. Eased into the channel by tugs, she made her way past the banana piers of the old city, the remains of Fort Sumter, past the break wall, the sea buoy, and moved on into deep water, on a course set for the English channel.

The voyage was to take two weeks, but it would end up taking one day longer because of an incident that took place outside the crew's messhall after supper the first evening. It happened while Yoya, the fifty-year-old Puerto Rican chief cook, was telling a number of bored Able-Bodied seamen why he did not kill rabbits anymore.

That no one cared bothered Yoya not at all. Yoya frequently told stories no one wanted to hear. Last night it had been Roberto Clemente's plane crash and the hammerhead sharks. By tomorrow he would be into the D.T.'s, preaching on the evils of prostitution—a favorite subject—and waving the meat cleaver. The leitmotif of these performances was "gonna cut off your balls and serve 'em for breakfast." But tonight he was in heaven, on the last of his rum, in one of his Family of Man moods, and telling how he came to love rabbits. First, though, it was important everyone understand *how* to kill rabbits. He illustrated his technique, gripping an invisible rabbit by the neck and smashing it repeatedly in the nose with the butt of a knife.

9

"You know *duwadeno?*" he asked. No one did.

"De olcer. I almos' focking *die*. Dey put me *tree feet* of *focking rabbit* duwadeno." He waited for a reaction which did not come. It was not really surprising that Yoya's duodenum had been replaced. That he still had his original kidneys was. He was about to expound on other matters of like significance when the commotion began outside the mess in the passageway.

McGowan, a twenty-two-year-old messman from Norfolk, was lying on the floor in a puddle by the ice machine, groaning and gritting his teeth. Crewmen hovered over him. "Don't touch him, don't touch him, it may be his spine. Get the Captain."

The Steward went up to get him.

Someone asked McGowan, "What happened?"

"My . . . back."

Marty, the third cook, mopped up the ice puddle which was trickling under the boy's back. The Steward's voice preceded him down the passageway.

"Here come de Cop'n! Here come de Cop'n!"

Captain Digby Lee, fifty-six, thick black hair combed almost straight up, pudgy in powder-blue polyester jumpsuit, rounded the corner. He leaned over McGowan.

"What happened?"

"Back. My back."

"Can you move?"

McGowan was going unconscious. The Captain shouted to bring him back.

"Can you move?"

He could move, but not much. The Captain checked his pupils, looking for dilation that would indicate pressure on the brain. McGowan moaned that he'd slipped and hit his spine against the handrail. Able-Bodied and Ordinary seamen deckhands arrived with the Stokes stretcher. They lifted him into it, with a gentleness incongruous with their faces. Unfortunately, they couldn't put him in the "hospital," a steel hut built out on the poop deck near the stern of the ship, because it would have meant walking in the dark across a rolling deck covered with oil. The seas were now about ten feet. The hospital wasn't much of a hospital anyway; over the years it had become more of a storage area for heavy iron rods, drums of lube oil, and big sections of plate glass lashed against the bunks, with edges to cut deep if a wave threw a man against them. So he had to be put in his own bunk.

If there had been serious injury to his spine, the descent two flights to the crew quarters would most likely have made him a quadriplegic. No funeral procession in the Roman catacombs ever was more difficult than the getting of two-hundred-pound McGowan down those narrow stairs and into his berth. It took eight men. McGowan was strapped into the mesh stretcher and when they tilted him upright to maneuver around corners, his head sagged. Twice he cried out in pain. When they reached his berth, they tried to slide him in the way pizzas are put into ovens, using a four-by-six-foot piece of plywood as a spatula. That did not work. So they locked arms under him and finally got him, groaning, onto the saggy mattress.

Slim wanted to get McGowan undressed, but McGowan said not to touch him just yet. He was all too conscious, and in agony. He wanted to rest. The Captain said he was going to go up and get Sparks to reach the Public Health station. He turned to Charley Fogarty, the chief mate, who was also the ship's chief medical officer. Charley Fogarty was a slight man, almost seventy, who wore wire-rimmed spectacles and had a face that seemed always on the verge of a grin—a grin that suggested he knew something you didn't, for which you were probably not better off.

"Chief, you better get his blood pressure and temperature and bring 'em up to me in the radio room," the Captain said.

"I don't know that we *have* a thermometer," the Chief Mate said matter-of-factly, as if the Captain had asked him for an astrolabe.

The Captain stood there a second, expression blank, enormous black eyebrows gathering the energy to furrow. This thermometer business was just the sort of thing that drove him crazy. He went up to see Sparks in the radio room.

Slim and some of the younger crewmembers—Rocco, Cascabel—stayed with McGowan. Gut brought down a plastic garbage bag full of ice and wedged it against McGowan's kidneys, as close as possible to his spine. Scabs were forming on McGowan's knuckles; someone asked if he wanted ice there too.

"Naw," said McGowan, "that's from a month ago. Three guys jumped me. *Two* guys, really. Damn, it was just beginnin' to heal, too." The scabs had opened during a fight the previous night. Five minutes before the lines were taken in, McGowan had come up the gangway wobbly, bloodstained, and broke. His hair was still matted with blood and the fourteen-stitch scar running from the back of his ear to his collarbone was orange from Mercurochrome. It was the loss of blood and the shock that had made him pass out by the ice machine.

He'd gone to a place in the black part of town called the Flying Dutchman, a place with a rough reputation, to buy some hash. He asked around and eventually someone said he could help him; even offered him a ride back to the ship. They'd stop and pick up the hash on the way. McGowan accepted the ride. Then the man pulled the car over to a schoolyard. McGowan said:

"All of a sudden he's beatin' me on the side of the head with a heavy screwdriver, the sharp end. And then this other guy appears and he's kickin' me in the head and face. Then this *third* guy appears. I'm punchin' and kickin' but it's lookin' pretty bad. I broke free and took out my wallet and held it up and said, '*You want the fuckin' money? Here, take it.*' An' threw it down on the ground and took off. But the first guy is still chasin' me, about four blocks. My face's all covered with blood so I couldn't see real well. He was right behind me. And I took off my shirt. I threw it at him and said, 'You want the damn shirt too?' I started to think, *Aw, damn, my girl friend gave me that shirt and she's always sayin' as how I lose things.* So he bent over to pick it up and while he was doing that I run and caught him right in the face with my foot. I think I heard his nose break."

"Yeah?" said Slim.

"Yeah. Then the other two come runnin' up and I had to take off. I stopped at some house. Old people. I banged on the door and this old lady comes to it. I said, 'Please, ma'am, I am sorry for disturbin' you like this but may I use your phone to call

12

the police?' She said, 'You'd better come in.' 'Cause I had all this blood on me. Police come and took me to the hospital and I told them who done it. They even got one of the guys."

But there was no time to go down and press charges. The ship was sailing. He had to get on it. He'd been waiting for a job almost three months. Shipping was bad. McGowan stared at the bedsprings of the upper bunk and looked like he wanted to cry.

Slim said, "They wasn't tough. *You* was tough. They was three o' them. One o' you." Rocco Lini, the second electrician, nodded, and said woe to those three meatballs if *he* ever ran into them.

"Mike," Slim said to McGowan, "I was *worried.* See, I *knew* you was goin' to the black part of town. That black girl come pick you at th' dock? I know her. You like that smoked meat, huh?"

McGowan snorted and blushed. "Yeah, it's okay."

"I tol' that girl while you was gettin' ready t'go, I tol' her, 'I gonna be comin' *back* to Charleston and this boy my *frien'.* So don't be messin' with 'im. Then, at three, when you wasn't back, I call the place. The Dutchman. And they say you haven' been there for coupla hours."

Slim had paced up and down the dock for what was left of the night, waiting for McGowan to come back to the ship. Slim was not violent by nature, but now he told Mike he wanted to go there with an ax next time.

Sparks and the Captain were hunched over a thick book, and enveloped in the cumulus of Pall Mall smoke that was Sparks's trademark atmosphere. The doctor who came on board in Charleston to give everyone a physical the day before she sailed hadn't liked the sound of Sparks's cough. He listened closely with the stethoscope.

"You smoke heavy?" he asked.

Sparks shuffled his feet. "Well, regular." (Two to three packs a day for forty-five years.)

"You've got emphysema," the doctor said. "You ought to have tests."

Sparks didn't want to have any tests. He stayed aboard, after the doctor left, coughing and scoffing and trying to convince himself and others it was nonsense. "How the hell can he tell I got emphysema just listening with the stethoscope? Tell me that."

Sparks had been at sea since he was seventeen. With his white hair, sunken chest, spindly arms, thick, black-rimmed glasses, and white T-shirt, he was like some kind of wireless jockey hunched over his transmitter. He was good, the kind of man who'd stay on the key until the ship went down. Radio telegraphy had changed considerably since he had shipped out with the navy forty-two years ago. Now a thick book listed the right acronyms for everything. In real emergencies, the old ones—SOS, CQD—were still used, but in situations like this, there was Procedure. He looked through the book.

"Here it is, Captain," Sparks finally said. "SITCASREP. Aw, shit, lookit all this." The directions for sending in a Situation Casualty Report were a page long.

The Captain turned to Cascabel, one of the Able-Bodied seamen.

"The Chief found that thermometer yet?"

"No, sir, I believe he's still looking for it."

"One of these days—"

"Sir?"

"Nothin'. Okay, I'll be down. I gotta check McGowan's pupils. How's he feeling?"

"Poorly, sir."

Cascabel walked down four decks to McGowan's focscle. Slim was still tending to McGowan, talking about football. Rocco was telling the others something about riding a skateboard with a flamethrower on his back during his navy Special Forces training. Cascabel told McGowan it was taking a little time to find the right form for relaying medical information back to U.S. Public Health Service. Slim shook his head.

"It's a *bad* life, man," he said.

"Dog's life," said McGowan.

"Yeah, but more money than anywhere else," Rocco said quickly.

The Captain eventually came in, shooed the crowd out, and told McGowan not to worry, that Sparks was on to Public Health, and the ship wasn't far from the coast. He told McGowan to rest easy and try not to move.

"Honest to God, Captain," said McGowan, "I didn't mean to be this much trouble to you."

"I know you didn't," said the Captain, who looked at McGowan's pupils with a flashlight. He had three boys McGowan's age. His manner was fatherly. Fogarty, the chief mate, arrived with a thermometer—a rectal thermometer.

"Real great, Chief," said the Captain, flushing. "How you suppose we gonna move a man with a spine injury to take his temperature?"

"Well—"

"Never mind. Just take his other vital signs and bring 'em up to me in the radio officer's room." He left. The Chief smiled an enigmatic smile. He said to Cascabel, "You take his pulse." Cascabel complied, though he had no experience at taking pulses.

"What else?" he asked the Chief.

"Does he feel hot?"

He did.

"Can he move?"

He could. It was clear Fogarty did not want to get personally involved.

"How's he feel?"

"How you feeling, Mike?"

"Like shit."

"He feels like shit, Chief."

The SITCASREP finally went into USPHS. There were hours of back and forth about pupil dilation, increasingly persistent requests for the patient's specific temperature ("Tell them it's above normal, just tell them that," the Captain told Sparks), the pulse rate, and more. The Captain stayed up all night. Just after 3:00 A.M., he checked McGowan's pupils again, and they looked dilated. Sparks radioed in the information, and Public Health finally wired back that this might indicate brain hemorrhaging. The Captain ordered the ship to turn back. Her course was swung

15

around, toward North Carolina. The Captain got the Coast Guard to make arrangements for an evacuation.

Outside, toward dawn of what was now Thanksgiving Day, the air was clear, with a light breeze and a gentle swell out of the north. McGowan was dozing, so Slim went aft to perch on the taffrail, have a smoke, and watch the stars disappear. Slim hadn't been on board two days and was already wishing he were back home in Norfolk.

"You know," he said in his Norfolk accent, "I *hate* bein' out here. I hate goin' t'sea." The closest he ordinarily got was long-shore work, but since his father was aboard the *Columbianna* as chief steward, here he was. Most children of merchant mariners grow up strangers to their fathers.

"He ain' never been home for my birthday," said Slim, "an' I'm twenny-*five*. Ain' never seen me play football. The one birthday he was home for he was so badly burned—that was the time he had the hot grease thrown on 'im by that cook—he couldn't do nothin'. 'Cause he was in pain the whole time. He only just settle that business befo' this trip. I think the lawyer got 'im a hunnerd and twenny-five thousand dollars. Get him t'show you his scar. Man who done it to him, I don' think he serve no time. Maybe they take his papers away from him for a while o' some-thin'. I believe he still sailin'. That's when my daddy *really* start drinkin'." He laughed. "Well, my daddy *always* been drinkin'. He was drunk when it happen. Doctor at the Public Health told him he woulda died for sure, from the shock, if he hadn' been drunk at the time. It was this big pan of boilin' chicken fat. Said he woulda died. The thang no one know is he didn' pass out right away. He pass out in the hallway on his way down to his cabin to get his gun to shoot that cook."

Slim looked down. "He still drinkin', my daddy. He say he gonna drink less this trip, maybe 'cause I'm here. He say he throw his whiskey overboard yesterday comin' outa Charleston. Well, he *say* he throw his whiskey overboard. Sometimes what my daddy *say* ain' what he *do.*"

In his cabin, just after dawn, the Captain was getting ready to shave. He was shaking his head.

16

"Chief Steward wouldn't turn to," he said. "Had to go down and chew his ass out. Then he come up and tell me the cook won't turn to. Now I gotta go down chew *his* ass out."

When he stopped by the radio room ten minutes later, little squares of toilet paper were stuck to his cheeks. The Captain cut himself almost every morning. He had a coarse beard, and in his enormous, meaty hands—he wore a size-seventeen ring—his safety razor was a play toy, miniature and unwieldy. He couldn't adjust to electric shavers and so was reconciled to this quotidian bloodletting.

Sparks, his wavy white hair still mussed from a half-hour nap, had been listening to Armed Forces Radio.

"They took over another one of our embassies last night," he announced with the matter-of-factness of one too long at sea. If nuclear war had broken out, Sparks would have reported it with equal bemusement.

"But get this," he said, "George McGovern's calling for force in Cambodia. George McGovern. What's going *on* here?"

These were interesting times. The day before the *Columbianna* sailed from Charleston, the Shiite Moslems had taken over a mosque in Mecca. The news on TV had sounded dire: the *Kitty Hawk* and the *Midway* were reported en route to the Mediterranean, and all U.S. forces were on something called DefCon Three. Low level, but an alert.

That night, in order to sneak a few cases of beer aboard—booze is theoretically not allowed on U.S. merchant vessels—one man created a diversion by shouting "Engine Room Supplies," while the others lugged cases past the two guards at the gate. Higgin, an Able-Bodied seaman, chatted up another set of guards, asking them what the latest news was. Was the U.S. at war yet?

"I tell you, sonny," said the older of the two guards, "I fought in the Second World War, but I'd volunteer *tomorrow.*"

"I'm with you, Mr. Dill," said the younger one.

" 'Bout time to start kickin' that Ayatollah in 'is ass."

Sparks's news about another embassy falling thus unsettled the Captain, who was beginning to wonder what the *Columbianna*'s role in all this geopolitical lunacy would be. Earlier this

17

year he'd spent two miserable weeks in Bandar-e Shahpur, one of Iran's major ports, trying to get his cargo unloaded while mobs ran through the streets. One week after the *Columbianna* pulled in, the Shah left on a "vacation" that ended up permanent. It was not a good time to be the only American ship in Iran. The ship's agent, a gentle old man named Mr. Mobasser, was shot in the stomach, then later dragged from his hospital bed, and impaled on a spike in the town square. Every day, two holy men came down to the ship, which was under Iranian armed guard, to drink 7-Ups with the Captain and ask penetrating questions like, "How do you feel about Islam?"

The Captain, a plainspoken man from Missou*ra*, as he pronounced it, told them that, oh, he was *quite* interested in Islam. (He had recently run across a British sailor just discharged from the local hospital. During his stay there, some Iranians had come by his bed, pointed a .45 at his head, cocked it, and asked, "You are American?" The Briton had started speaking Norwegian— "with some fluency," he told the Captain.

The whole experience had been one nightmare after another. "The average age of my crew was sixty," the Captain said. "There was this messman, son of a bitch named Rasheed Abdullah somethin'r other, who signed on in Brooklyn. He was a Moslem. He was a white fellah, but he was a Moslem. Ever time I looked down there, he's on the dock yak-yakkin' away with the guards. I told everybody I didn't even want 'em leavin' the ship. They got troops walkin' up and down with bayonets. Ol' Rasheed come back up the gangway real cocky and says to me, 'Captain, I can have anyone on the ship killed for a quarter.' I told him, 'You do and you'll be the second one to go.' "

The Captain shook his head. "I coulda kicked his ass."

The odd part of it was the Iranians came to suspect that the messman was a CIA agent, and the Captain finally had to convince the holy men not to pull him off the ship.

"It was one revoltin' development after another, I tell ya," he said. "Everything I could think of all ended one way—me gettin' hung."

The day the Captain finally got the go-ahead from Washington

18

to pull out, his seventy-eight-year-old third mate—a White Russian married to a twenty-eight-year-old Chinese acrobat—came running up to his cabin waving a telegram shouting, "We made it! We made it! Flash!" (Cables from the Pentagon are preceded by four designations, according to priority: Routine, Intermediate, Flash, and Flash Override. Higgin, the AB who knew about these sorts of communications from having served on nuclear submarines, said Flash Override "is where you have Almighty God saying, 'Disregard my last message.' ")

So on *this* Thanksgiving Day, 1979, the following were on the Captain's mind: an injured messman with possible brain damage; a drunk steward and cook who wouldn't turn to; a saltwater leak in the number one condenser; and a complex gale system moving down from the northeast. On top of this he had a feeling in his gut that Sparks would soon be handing him a telegram from the company, saying:

PROCEED PERSIAN GULF PENDING INSTRUCTIONS

What a revoltin' development *that* would be.

Yoya and the steward sweated over Thanksgiving lunch. The Captain had chewed them out to some effect, and their efforts, though more of a forced march than a labor of love, were successful. Yoya's hands were shaking from the DTs. When a gallon tin of cranberry sauce refused to open, he let out a *puta maricón coño carrajo cabrón puta puta puta modderfocker!* Marty, the frail, patient third cook, being nearest, was the chief object of Yoya's tirades. Before daybreak, Yoya made Marty haul all the frozen turkeys and sides of pork and lamb out of the meat locker by himself. It was a pitiful sight. Marty had been torpedoed during the war, spent time in a German POW camp, and looked not significantly healthier now than he did the day he was released. Pyorrhea made the smile that he only infrequently managed a little ghastly. His spine was hunched, as if in confirmation of his lot. He drank as heavily as he could, but because he shared a focsle with Yoya, he had to drink furtively—otherwise Yoya would

19

appropriate it for himself. Slim and his friend Gut felt sorry for Marty and helped him with the turkeys and other frozen meats.

By 11:30 A.M. the mess tables were spread with basted birds, steaming potatoes, creamed onions, radishes, hard-boiled eggs, chestnuts, mince pies, pumpkin pies, apple pies, cookies, turnips, roast lamb, pork ribs, pitchers of cold cider, candies, plum puddings, fresh milk, hard candies, hot biscuits, and eggnog full of brandy. The officers did not drink any eggnog—since the ship was only hours away from a mid-ocean rendezvous with a Coast Guard helicopter—but everyone else left the mess with lips caked yellow. It was a feast. As a gesture of appreciation, one of the Able-Bodied seamen slipped Yoya a half-gallon bottle of Bacardi.

Shortly after lunch, just as the men had stretched out and would otherwise have enjoyed a good, long, lazy holiday afternoon, the order to turn to—that is, to start working—came down from the Captain's office, and preparations were begun for the helicopter evacuation. The ship was now within range of the mainland. The Bosun, the man in charge of the deck crew, rounded up his ABs and Ordinaries. (The deck crew consists of Able-Bodied and Ordinary seamen. An AB is supposed to be competent to perform any task except engineering and navigation. An Ordinary is not required to climb rigging. The Coast Guard insists that an Ordinary have one year of sailing before he can sit for his AB examination.)

Five or six men went below to bring poor McGowan topside. The rest busied themselves clearing away cables that might catch the helicopter's prop.

The men were in elevated spirits as they wedged McGowan back into the Stokes stretcher. McGowan himself had been given a whack or two at the eggnog, so he didn't mind the trip up as much as he had the one down. He had not been overjoyed at the prospect of being lifted off the deck by a steel cable hanging from a helicopter, but now the more he thought about it, the better he felt.

"Do me a favor when you get there," J.D., the Ordinary, said to him on the way up. "Call my wife and tell her I ain't never comin' home."

The Captain ordered the men to put McGowan down on the number four cargo hold hatch cover, just forward of the superstructure, thinking the helicopter would need maneuvering space. The trouble was the king posts. Two of these Vs towered over the number four. Some very precise flying would be necessary to get between them. McGowan took stock of this plan and said he thought it was the "horriblest" idea he'd ever heard, and said his back was suddenly feeling a lot better. Tom Dexter, the old third mate, came down; gave it a lookover with his wise eyes, and suggested they use the poop deck. The Captain agreed with Mr. Dexter, as he always did. McGowan was lugged back to the stern, the poop deck was cleared, the rusted flagpole lowered (in a reverse Iwo Jima tableau, five men struggling to wrench Old Glory down) and everyone stood by and waited for the United States Coast Guard.

The Captain had them on the VHF but couldn't see them yet. The bridge was 68 feet over the water, and from that height, on a clear day, the horizon is 9.4 miles away. The Search and Rescue helicopter was headed for the point of rendezvous, 180 miles southeast of Cape Hatteras, North Carolina. That spot was at the outer limit of the helicopter's fuel range, so a C-130 flew ahead of it, to guide it in with no waste of time or loss of fuel. Somewhere below the horizon about $20 million worth of technological cavalry was homing in on the *Columbianna*.

The VHF conversation between the Captain, in his Missoura drawl, and the commander of the rescue mission, in his best Chuck Yeager accent, sounded like this:

CAPTAIN: You want us to change course or anything?

COAST GUARD: Ah, that's a negative, sir. When you have us in sight we are a white helicopter with an orange stripe. When you have us in sight please give us a call. That will help us locate you. We think we may have you on radar here.

CAPTAIN: Roger that. We're keepin' a good lookout for you.

COAST GUARD: Thank you, sir. Could you give me a quick short count?

CAPTAIN: Ah, zero, one, two, three, four, five, five, four, three, two, one. Over.

COAST GUARD: Very fine, very fine. That'd make it about

21

sixteen miles yet. We're northwest of you at three three zero magnetic.

"There he is," said Mr. Darby, the blond, twenty-two-year-old third mate, who was standing by the radar screen. The *Columbianna* carried two third mates.

CAPTAIN: *Columbianna* to Medevac, ah, we got a little blip here on our radar. Probably that is you. Over.

COAST GUARD: Roger dodger. Probably that is us. We are indicating a blip on our radar too, about sixteen miles away at this time. We'll see you shortly, Captain.

The C-130 broke the horizon first and in minutes passed astern, buzzing two hundred feet over the water. It made slow circles around the ship while the helicopter caught up like a fat bumblebee. It came up over the poop deck very slowly. The Chief Mate yelled, "Don't touch the basket till they lower the grounding wire—you'll get electrocuted." (If you grab a cable dangling from a helicopter before the cable has touched the ground, the electrical current generated by its engines can kill you.) The *tupatupatupatupatupa* of the rotor blades, now fifteen feet above the poop deck, swept away every loose bit of dirt, tar, salt, rag, fuzz, lint, rust, butts, scum, slops, grease, soot, and sea-gull droppings. The poop deck was never again so clean. McGowan, lying in the stretcher, alone, directly beneath the source of the maelstrom, had his sunglasses stripped off his face and his Louis L'Amour paperback blown away. The grounding wire touched the deck, and down dropped a corpsman in a bright orange flight suit.

COAST GUARD: Okay, Captain, looks like we got a good contact there. We're gonna have another look-see before the hoist.

CAPTAIN: Ah, very good.

COAST GUARD: During the hoist situation the pilot will be off frequency so you can talk to me and there'll be no problem. Over to you.

CAPTAIN: Okay. Mighty fine.

The corpsman checked McGowan's vital signs, helped transfer him into a Coast Guard stretcher, covered him up, and strapped him in.

22

"Wait a minute," said McGowan. "Where's my book?" It was found ten feet away, wedged under a chock. The Bosun slipped it into the stretcher. The corpsman signaled to the helicopter, now hovering twenty yards astern. Everyone stood back as it crept up cautiously over the poop, blade tips four feet from a cargo boom. The hook dropped and, with an amok vibration, lifted the boy with dilated pupils off the ship into the sky.

CAPTAIN: Kilo Papa Golf Quebec calling Coast Guard.

Long pause.

COAST GUARD: Ah, roger, Kilo Papa, we were off frequency there. Ah, your people did a nice job. Is there anything else we can do for you heading back to Elizabeth City?

CAPTAIN: Thank you, ah, that's very considerate of you. You helped us out considerably and I guess you folks can take better care of the patient than we can.

COAST GUARD: Okay, Captain, nice to work with you. We'll be hooking up some other time. Have a happy Thanksgiving— what's left of it. This is copter one four three seven clear and out with the *Columbianna.*

At 3:54 P.M., local time, the moment the helicopter lifted off, the course was set once more for the English channel. The Captain went to his office to do the figuring. The eight-and-a-half hour diversion cost the company about $3,200, plus another $3,-000 in fuel: including the holiday premium overtime, it would all come out to about $9,000.

"There's gonna be some bitchin' and moanin' at the front office," the Captain said. Thirty-six years at sea had made him tired. He shrugged: *"Whaddya* gonna do?"

Human error, frailty, mental fatigue, idiocy, storms, corruption, illness, coffee stains on the bridge, union dues, theft, madness, collision, war, taxes, Iranian holy men—it was all part of the *"Whaddya* gonna do?" It was his gestalt. He would have left the sea a long time ago, but he knew nothing else. And now he had three boys approaching college age, and bills. He rubbed his eyes. At least the airlift had gone smoothly. The last time he'd done it, it had been a case of epilepsy off Cape Town. His crew had

had to wrestle the seaman, who was kicking and foaming at the mouth, into the Stokes.

"I tell you," he said, raising one heavy eyebrow, "that was a *real* bearcat."

Several hours after the helicopter had come and gone, Chief Engineer Muzzio was in the Captain's office insisting the ship be diverted into Bermuda. "Chiefy" was in his mid-fifties, balding, wiry, frenetic, and wide-eyed. He was always wide-eyed. He had a hard time sitting still. Though he should have run out of adrenaline years ago, still it permeated his system.

There was a saltwater leak in the number one condenser, true; but repairs could take days. Chiefy—the nickname the Chief Engineer preferred over his other, "the Village Idiot"—had sent a telegram through Sparks to Mr. Dodd, recommending they put in for repairs anyway. Mr. Dodd, company vice-president in charge of engineering, was bound to be *real* pleased about that, the Captain said.

The Captain and Chiefy loathed each other, had for nine years, ever since they both joined the company and began working on the *Columbianna*. They had been trying to get each other fired for the last eight-and-a-half. With each successive failure, their mutual disregard was augmented. By now each was convinced the other "had something" on the company. The Captain looked at the copy of the telegram Sparks had dropped off on his desk:

UNABLE TO STOP SALTWATER LEAK WITH SAWDUST MAIN CONDENSER STOP RECOMMEND STOPPING BERMUDA FOR REPAIRS STOP PLEASE ADVISE SOONEST STOP ETA NOW APPROX 1800 LOCAL 22ND

SIGNED CH. ENG. MUZZIO

The Captain went up to the chart room to see if he had a Bermuda harbor chart, and found that he didn't. What he had was a chart of the entire North Atlantic, with as much detail of the Bermuda shoals as a map showing everything from the state of Georgia to the Pyrenees. Landing at JFK using a Rand

McNally roadmap of the eastern United States would be roughly analogous. "Bamboola, Bamboola," he said softly, staring at the chart spread out beneath him.

He had been mate once, he explained, on a Liberty ship crossing the North Atlantic. "The skipper was just about eighty years old," he said. "It was his last trip. I don't know if maybe he had orders to sink her for insurance or what, but he set the course right for those shoals off the north tip of Bermuda. Right for those rocks. The old Chinese steward—he was kind of excitable, you know—come runnin' down to me sayin', 'Mate! Mate! *Bamboola! Bamboola!* This close!' " The Captain held his thumb and forefinger a hairbreadth apart. "I went up onto the bridge, into the navigation room, and changed the course. An hour later I checked the wheel, see, and the skipper had changed it back. So I'd go change it again, and he'd change it again. Well, I tell you, this went on quite a while, and we weren't gettin' any further away from old Bamboola. But I wasn't crazy about goin' up on the rocks, so I went back up and changed it *real* good and just stayed there on the bridge till we was clear of Bamboola." The Captain looked up from the chart. "I don't know, really. Maybe he was sorta tired and sick with it all."

Mrs. Wilson's
Burden

ONE DAY IN MID-ATLANTIC A TANKER APPEARED ON THE HORIZON and passed close enough for her name to be read through binocs. She was the *Overseas Vivian,* a wide-bellied lady of forty thousand tons deadweight.

Higgin, smoking on the poop deck, watched her and wondered how ships came by names like that. Higgin loved to talk about and speculate about nautical lore. Part of it was his southernness, his love of language and metaphor; the rest resulted from his having been at sea since he was seventeen—*under* the sea, mostly, in submarines. He was thirty-one now and had been in the merchant marine less than a year. He was the only man aboard —maybe the only Able-Bodied seaman in the world—who went ashore dressed in tweed jackets, ties, penny loafers, and blue and pink cotton button-down shirts. He had thinning blond hair, companionable blue eyes behind gold wire-rimmed glasses, and table manners.

"Imagine," said Higgin, squinting into the sun, "if she were captured by Cambodian or North Korean gunboats, everyone shouting, 'Free the *Overseas Vivian!*' " They decided *Columbianna* would make a far better battle cry.

She came by the name circuitously. The *Columbianna's* original name, the *Marine Bobcat,* was a war-issue special. All C-4 troop ships were given names of fish, birds, or animals, with an occasional fruit or mythic beast thrown in, all prefixed with

Marine; as in *Marine Adder, Leopard, Raven, Swallow, Dragon,* and *Peach.* In 1968, under new ownership and fitted with the cockroach legs that would have looked silly on a bobcat, she was rechristened, in part after the Columbia River, on whose banks she had been built, and in which she was laid up for ten years, under the shadow of Mount Saint Helens. The river itself, discovered by Robert Gray in 1792, was named for his ship. Some of America's most distinguished ships have been named *Columbia:* the first U.S. vessel to circumnavigate the globe; the yachts that defended the America's Cup in 1899, 1901, and 1958. NASA chose the name for its most ambitious craft, the Space Shuttle. So as it was, the S.S. *Columbianna* was named for a river named after a ship named after a new land named for an Italian navigator.

Many of America's famous ships have had distinctively American names: *Manhattan, Savannah, Mayaguez, Pueblo.* The CIA's Russian sub-catcher was named *Glomar Explorer.* Richard Henry Dana sailed to California, an almost unknown land, on the brig *Pilgrim,* and came back worldly wise on the *Alert.* Melville signed on as boy aboard the packet ship *St. Lawrence,* later on the whaler *Acushnet, Lucy Ann, Charles and Henry;* finally on the man-of-war *United States.* Nelson Algren crossed the Pacific with a trunkful of Hemingway books on the *Malaysia Mail.* Hart Crane committed suicide leaping into the Caribbean off the freighter *Orizaba.* One of the last fully rigged American sailing ships was called *Tusitala,* "teller of tales," the name given Robert Louis Stevenson by the South Seas natives.

Some of the American merchant ships afloat today have romantic, evocative names: the *Achilles, African Dawn, Arcturus, Sugar Islander, Tallulah, Jeff Davis, Vermillion, Virgo, Poet* (she went down with all hands in the North Atlantic, in November 1980), *Traveller, Trinity, Zapata Rover.* On the other hand, there are the *Carbide Seadrift, El Paso Arzew, Neches, Exxon Newark* (Worst Name in Fleet), *Magoffin, LA/ACA, Delta Sud,* and the *AP-127.* The names of the liquefied natural gas carriers—state-of-the-art American merchant ships—are fusions of acronyms and the heavens: *LNG Aquarius, LNG Capricorn, LNG Taurus,* etc.

There are fifteen tankers called *Texaco North Dakota, Texaco New Jersey* (Second Worst Name in Fleet), and so on. The trend these days is toward the literal. Ships are named for their function or cargo. Thus, on a windswept day in the Straits of Malacca, you may come across the *Seabulk Magnachem,* or the *Socony Vacuum,* a Mobil tanker. Another tanker, the *Pure Oil,* would seem to be a paradigm of the trend.

Historically, finding names for American ships has been a problem. Edith Bolling Wilson, wife of the president, had a hard time of it during World War I. The U.S. shipping board constantly asked her to name new ships. She used names of lakes, rivers, cities, mountains, and even then ran out, finally resorting to virtually unpronounceable Indian names such as *Shickshinny, Tobesofka,* and *Sisladobsis.* The press was much amused and gave her all sorts of hell. Having just finished with eighty-eight German vessels commandeered in U.S. ports, she was asked to name a few hundred new merchant ships. Years later she wrote in her autobiography, "Trivial as it may seem, as the War went on, and other duties increased, this work of naming ships became a genuine burden."

During World War II, when the United States built an amazing 3,876 new merchant ships—almost seven times the number in the present U.S. flag fleet—naming them, as well as the new war ships, was not at all easy. With all the good submarine names already taken, one navy bureaucrat was reduced to "scrabbling around for names like *Spinax, Irex, Merd,* and *Sirago.*" He named one sub *Trepang* and later found out the trepang is a sea slug. The man in charge of naming ships during World War II, Capt. William T. Calkins, found that "even reaching into the heavens was not safe," as he discovered when he almost named one ship after a star an astronomer had named for the poodle of his mistress. In sharp contrast, the British submarine *Varangian* took its name from the Norse bodyguard of the Byzantine emperor.

During the Spanish-American War, the navy got the idea to honor American colleges, and so two ships were rechristened the *Yale* and the *Harvard.* After Admiral Dewey captured the Spanish fleet in the Battle of Manila, he received orders to give the ships collegiate names. He wired back two proposals: *Massachusetts Institute of Technology* and *Vermont Normal College for Women.* Washington got the message and the admiral was not asked for further suggestions; but the idea was still alive two wars later, with the *Harvard Victory, Wesleyan Victory,* and—most unmistakably—the *C.C.N.Y. Victory.*

One of Winston Churchill's great pleasures as First Lord of the Admiralty in World War I was naming ships, though King George V had final approval. On one occasion, Churchill proposed names for three new ships: the *Assiduous, Liberty,* and *Oliver Cromwell.* His Majesty thought *Assiduous* would "invite ribald nicknames," that *Liberty* was a common term for libertine, and that the third name, that of history's most notorious anti-monarchist, was positively unamusing. Churchill came back with *Marlborough* (his own ancestor) and *Emperor of India,* but he would not give up on *Cromwell.* Cromwell had heavily built up England's navy, and Churchill felt he deserved the recognition. He suggested the name three more times, His Majesty growing more and more piqued. Churchill eventually sent a message to the king saying, "It certainly seems right that we should give to a battleship a name that never failed to make the enemies of England tremble." The king, it is recorded, "stood grimly firm."

Politics has always played its role. The earliest known ship name, belonging to a large cedarwood Egyptian vessel at the time of Snefru about 2920 B.C., was *Praise of the Two Lands.* This name was intended to stress geopolitical unity between the quarrelsome North and South kingdoms. After the revolutionary engagements at Concord and Lexington, Massachusetts launched the sloop *Tyrannicide. Rising States, United We Stand, Divided We Fall, Blockade, Fourth of July,* and others followed. During the Civil War, when the North was anxious to woo the Irish, the ship *Shamrock* was christened on Saint Patrick's Day with a bottle of Irish whiskey. The South, not to be outdone, named a submersible torpedo boat the *Saint Patrick.* To please South America during World War II, the United States named twelve Liberty ships after Latin heroes such as *Simon Bolivar, Bernardo O'Higgins,* and

30

others. The first black to command a U.S. ship was given charge of the *Booker T. Washington*. At one time, Spain decreed that every single Spanish ship had to have a religious name. Archbishop John Roach, on the other hand, thought "nearly sacrilegious" the U.S. Navy's naming, in December, 1981, its newest nuclear attack submarine the U.S.S. *Corpus Christi*. Secretary of the Navy Lehman explained it was being named only for the town in Texas, not for the Feast of Eucharist.

The Romans chose sober, imperial names. Nero sailed once on the *Augustus Carrier*. The Vikings, who christened their vessels by tying human victims to the logs they were launched down (a lovely practice known as "roller-reddening"), named their ships after *orms*, sea snakes, and mythic beasts. The point clearly was to terrorize—heads mounted on the prows were actually removed before coming into port so the homeland spirits would not be frightened. One of these vessels was called *The Ship One Must Beware Of*. In nearby literary waters, Billy Budd's H.M.S. *Bellipotent* was almost sunk engaging the French line-of-battle ship *Athee* (the *Atheist*), a name, wrote Melville, "proclaiming the infidel audacity of the ruling power," and, "though not so intended to be, the aptest name, if one considers it, ever given to a warship."

The word *freighter* itself is now on the way out. The new word is *brake-bulk*, the old term for opening and unloading the holds of ships. Brake-bulk means exactly what freighter means, but is considered more sophisticated, the way *facilitate* is thought by some to be superior to *ease*. In its copious pamphlets pleading with companies to ship their products on U.S. flag vessels, the National Maritime Council lobby defines a brake-bulk ship as "a noncontainerized general cargo ship," which is a bit of like defining radio by saying it is "nontelevision."

Many of today's ships are so highly specialized they require acronymic designations instead of the old classical ones such as Liberty or Hog Islander. By now everyone knows about ULCCs and VLCCs—respectively, Ultra Large and Very Large Crude Carriers—because they always seem to be ruining beaches and killing marine life, and because the next world war may start over their rights of passage through the Strait of Hormuz. Less well-known are the LASH ships, SEABEEs, LNGs, SL-7s, SL-18s, OBOs, and RO/ROs, many of which bear as much resemblance to older, traditional ships as a Winnebago camper does to a Conestoga wagon.

A ship, Henry Major Tomlinson wrote in *The Sea and the Jungle,* "has happenings according to her own weird. She shows perversities and virtues her parents never dreamed into the plans they laid for her." A few American merchant ships in the nineteenth century certainly bore this out. The *Tarry Not* sailed from Maine to Philadelphia with a cargo of Christmas trees, arriving shortly after Washington's birthday. *Big Bonanza,* a Downeaster, was sold four times for debt in thirteen years. *Brilliant Sailor* held the record for the longest transatlantic passage. In our own time, the ship *Cuba Victory* seems to have been prematurely christened.

When the *Columbianna* pulled into New Orleans later on in the voyage, she docked behind the *Samuel Chase,* an old Waterman freighter, built in 1953. Her rusted hull was the color of mid-October maple leaves. No one was aboard. The ship was a picture of neglect, cables frayed, decks soot caked, a starboard list she'd probably had for years. The docking lines were ancient, and whoever had put them there hadn't even bothered to attach the ratguards. A security man on the dock said she was on her way to the scrapyard up river at Todd's, to be broken down into razor blades. Higgin said he wouldn't want to shave with any blade from that sorry-looking old beast. No amount of smelting was going to get the tetanus out of *that* steel. The Chief Steward said it was a bad ship with a bad history—a couple of murders, one involving an ax. Real bloody ship. She'd been named after a patriot of the American Revolution, signer of the Declaration of Independence, justice of the Supreme Court, and a true gentleman, but her happenings had been strictly according to her own weird.

Pentland Firth

THE *COLUMBIANNA'S* TRANSATLANTIC COURSE RAN FROM Charleston to a point nineteen miles south of Santa Maria Island, in the Azores chain, and then cut north toward Lizard Point, England. From there up the channel, into the North Sea and Bremerhaven. This kept her south of the 35th two-thirds of the way. (During winters in the North Atlantic, navigators try to keep south of the 35th parallel, as most of the bad weather is north of it.) The Captain had plotted this course himself, preferring it to the one OTSR had recommended. OTSR stands for Optimum Track Ship Routing, a service provided by the navy to keep vessels away from bad weather. The Captain deeply mistrusted it. OTSR was always directing him through the Pentland Firth, the passage between the northernmost tip of Scotland and the Orkney Islands. The Pentland Firth was to him what Scylla and Charybdis were to Odysseus. He talked of jagged cliffs rising out of chaotic waters where the current ran ten knots. And whirlpools—big whirlpools—like the ones in Norway.

Ten years had passed since his last transit of the Firth. "What I remember of it," he said, looking glum, brows furrowed, "is a lot of rain and cold and unpleasantness." From Charleston to Bremerhaven via the Firth was shorter than the Captain's route by about half a day, it was true, and also had the advantage of a northerly lift from the Gulf Stream. But all that was nothing. It was the Pentland Firth that worried him. It was cold as hell up there this time of year, and rough, with Force Eight conditions prevailing half the time; icebergs too. He stabbed it on the chart with an enormous forefinger."I don't give a shit what they tell me," he said. "I ain't goin' through there."

There was another reason for his distrust of OTSR. He'd met a navy officer years back who'd worked there. "He told me 'bout this navy captain he had somethin' against. There was a woman involved. The guy told me, 'I routed that son of a bitch into every storm I could find.' Well, when I heard that, I tell ya, my ears went up like a jackrabbit."

The Chief Cook and Second Cook were both down with severe DTs, so they were excused from fire and lifeboat drill the day after Thanksgiving. Everyone else reported to his station. The Captain had a good reason for holding the weekly drills: "If I want to fire someone, and I haven't had no lifeboat drills, whoever it is I fire is gonna go to the Coast Guard and complain that the only drills I had were on paper, and pretty soon I'm up to my neck in shit."

Actually he took them more seriously than that. And he insisted that everyone wear a hat. "You go into a lifeboat without some kind of head protection, you're gonna be in pretty bad shape real soon with that sun beatin' down on you."

During World War II, a tanker captain, in waters off the tip of Greenland, received word a ship had been torpedoed in the area. There was scant chance of finding survivors, but he posted extra lookouts anyway. One of them sighted a half-dozen lifeboats. When the captain took the ship in close, he saw the men, in their underwear, sitting upright, frozen to the oars. They had lasted less than an hour. After that he gave orders that all men were to be fully dressed at all times, even while asleep. Any man found not fully clothed was fined a day's wages. To enforce the rule, he cut off the heat in the cabins.

Around noon Chief Engineer Muzzio—Chiefy—came running up the stairs. "Oh, man!" he yelled, even more wide-eyed than usual, "I'm *so fuckin'* happy! I'm *so fuckin'* happy!"

His men had stopped the saltwater leak in the condenser by sealing off half of it and isolating the source. All that remained was to plug it. The Captain expressed reserved satisfaction. He knew from the past nine years this was not really the end of it.

Sparks knocked on the Captain's cabin and handed Chiefy the telegram he had just received back from the company. It read: ISOLATE CONDENSER LEAK STOP USE COMMON SENSE STOP. This was Mr. Dodd's way of saying he expected no more telegrams about putting into Bamboola. Chiefy kept repeating, "I'm *so fuckin'* happy." This was his way of letting the Captain know he was being insufficiently grateful for the heroic, if not thaumaturgical, efforts of the engine-room gang. The Captain, though, said nothing. Finally Chiefy left to have a beer. The Captain's stare followed him out the door. "A good engineer has his fingers on two things, water and fuel," he said. He shook his head. "Well, he don't have his fingers on a goddam thing."

The next day OTSR, assuming the *Columbianna* was well on her way to the Pentland Firth, sent Sparks a message to divert south away from the Pentland Firth, because of a complex (more than one) gale system closing in on Newfoundland. On hearing this the Captain felt greatly vindicated. "See what I mean?" he said.

Pooch

As she approached the middle of the North Atlantic and the 35th parallel, the seas got rougher. The barometer fell steadily —though not as badly as it was falling off Newfoundland—and the Captain said by next morning there would be a good blow.

Gene Puchinelli was pacing the wing decks that stuck out on both sides of the bridge. "Pooch," as he was called, was forty-six. He had a high forehead and dark hair that curled forward onto his temples, giving him the look of a noble Roman bust. When he knitted his eyebrows, which he often did, it made him look less smart than he actually was. He talked all the time—*all* the time—and for this was thought a nuisance by the crew. He was a lonely man who had not had an easy life. He was an Able-Bodied seaman on the eight-to-midnight watch.

He flicked his cigarette off the deck, buttoned up his collar against the wind, and popped a Tagamet into his mouth. His stomach hurt. Three years ago his girl friend had stabbed him with a hunting knife, putting five punctures in his intestines. That was why he took Tagamet—to keep the acidity down. He had been talking without pause for an hour. A slice of moon hung low off the port quarter. Something in Pooch's monologue made him remember working on a ship that shuttled horses and cattle between Hawaii and San Francisco.

"It was so crowded," he said, "there was only one thing to do when a calf was born—throw it over the side. The weird thing

37

was you'd do everything you could to help with the birth. But there wasn't enough room. We had four or five of those. It'd break your heart."

Of the forty men on the *Columbianna*, almost half were orphans. Pooch himself was raised in a succession of brutal orphanages, contracting osteomyelitis at the age of seven from beatings on the shins, delivered by a nun with a dustpan. He finally made good his escape when he was thirteen.

In this regard seamen have not changed much since Melville's day. Melville found a lot of orphans adrift. They made up one of his central themes. From Arrowhead, his Massachusetts farm, Melville wrote to his friend Nathaniel Hawthorne, "The Godhead is broken like bread. We are the pieces." In the book he had recently finished, *Moby Dick,* he had written, "Our souls are like the children of those unwedded mothers who die in bearing them. The secret to our paternity lies in their graves, and we must there to learn it."

Pooch never knew his mother. That night on the wing deck he thought back to the time three years ago when a woman put a hunting knife into his belly and removed the one trace of maternity on him, his navel:

"It was in a bar right next to the house I live in, about two blocks away, and I'd just come back from the racetrack. Just ordered my first beer. I was with some of the guys from the racetrack. *She's* over on the right. That's why I didn't go over to the right. I could see she was as drunk as a skunk. Her and the barmaid were good friends. The barmaid didn't happen to be there that time of day. She was always telling that barmaid about us—good-looking barmaid, which by the way I had been sleeping with anyway, but that's neither here nor there. The owner was sleeping with her too.

"My girl friend was always trying to make the barmaid think I was madly in love with her, but she was just a place to hang my coat. So my girl friend said, 'Hey *dago*—dago!—you comin home with me tonight, honey?' Sloppy drunk, you know. I said, 'Leave me alone.' So she staggers down there, says, 'What's the matter, you lose all your money at the races?' I says, 'No.' 'You coming home with me tonight, honey?' When I get angry I don't say nothin', I just get quiet.

"She had a pocketbook in her hand. Apparently she had the knife behind her pocketbook. She says, 'You *sure* you not coming home tonight?' Real sweet pie. I says, 'No, leave me alone.' I turned my head, and she ran the knife right into my gut. I thought she *punched* me. When she pulled the knife out my guts came right out with it. Felt this terrible burning sensation. I grabbed for my guts. . . . It was a hunting knife. In other words, it was premeditated. She had planned it. You see, I hadn't been home in three nights. I had been shacked up with some other snake. 'Course she ran out the door, cause my immediate reaction was to give her a punch. But when she pulled it out I realized I was hurt.

"I went over to the bartender, my friend, and said, 'Fella, call the Lutheran ambulance.'

"He says, 'What for?'

"What for! You can see the guts hanging out, blood all over the place. He said, 'What's the number?' I said, 'Tell the fucking operator to make an emergency call.'

"So I lay on the floor, and of course the winos and drunks, they had all *kinds* of suggestions about what to do. I says, 'Get away from me, the ambulance'll be here.' One guy gave me an old raincoat to put my head on. I just lay on my side. About five minutes later they were there. Took me to the emergency. They wanted to know if I could pay for it. I said, 'I'm a merchant seaman, everything'll be paid for.' Then here come the cops and wanted to know who did it and all this. And I said, 'Don't worry about who did it, just sew me up.' They said, 'Well, you gotta tell us, you gotta sign this thing.' I says, 'I ain't gonna sign nothin'.' 'Suppose you die?' 'Well, then you're gonna have to do your job, that's all.'

"So they took all my clothes and my watch, and they had some medic or whatever he was look me over, and I felt sort of woozy. I says, 'Can you put the head of this bed up? I feel like —sick to my stomach.' So this dummy puts the head up. I figured

39

it had a locking device or something; you know those hospital beds, you crank 'em up. So he puts the head up. I says, 'Oh, yes, that's fine.' He lets go. The whole fucking thing drops. I could feel my stomach rip, just like that. By that time I'm throwing up all over the place. The nurse says, 'He's in shock.' But I was lucid. I felt cold stiff.

"I felt the razor blade. They were shaving me. Then they gave me a shot of something. I woke up at one o'clock in the recovery room. I had a tube in my nose, in my mouth. I was choking. I couldn't move, I couldn't move a muscle. All I could move was my eyes—up to here. I was on oxygen. I had a catheter in my peter, needles in both arms. Man, *am I alive?* But I could see the clock, 1:00 A.M. It was Easter Sunday.

"I was in that thing for four days. I was on the danger list for three days. I lost eleven pints of blood. She almost got the aorta.

"I didn't press charges. She had a couple of kids, you know. I figured, *What the hell? You put her in jail, and that ain't gonna heal the wound. And the kids'll go to an orphanage.* Well, anyway, at one o'clock in the morning when I woke up, I couldn't feel the pain. They had some good dope inside me. They got a heart machine on me. I look out of the corner of my eye and there *she* is—still drunk, cryin'. She must have doubled back. She went home, told her daughter that she'd killed me. She must have doubled back, found out the ambulance had taken me to Lutheran Hospital. She took a helluva chance cause the cops coulda still been there. She worked her way into that room—without permission or nothing. And now I got this ungodly fear she's comin' to finish the job. And I'm helpless. I can't move a muscle. This heart machine's making noises. If she hadn't shown up I would have felt a lot better. Here I got stitches on the aorta and the heart machine's going on and you could have busted a blastoma—what do you call it? What a hopeless situation. The nurse comes over and here the heart machine's going crazy and she says, 'You're all right now.' I go with my eyes—desperation—*get her out of here!* Then I spot the daughter. The daughter come over

40

to me. I knew I was all right then cause I knew she wouldn't do it to me with the daughter there. The daughter and I were pretty good buddies. Then I collapsed again.

"I woke up around five in the morning and she wasn't there . . . but every day she come to visit me, even when I got transferred up to the regular rooms there. She kept saying to me, 'You gonna come home afterward?' I said, 'Sure.' You know I'm not gonna say no in this condition. But I knew I wasn't going home to her.

"A doctor at Public Health said I have a manic-depressive-type personality. If I should go off the deep end, I would go into manic depression. This is what my father was. He was in a mental hospital.

"He's in Providence now. He just got out of the nut house two or three months ago. And—ironic twist of events—this year I was in Connecticut visiting some friends, and I'd driven in from Cleveland, and I just suddenly thought I'd take a ride out to Providence, see what it's looking like. So I did. Drove down there. Parked the car. Started walking around. I look up ahead of me and there's my father. Hadn't seen him in twenty-two years. Hadn't seen him since 1957, when I was just out of the service.

"He had a broken arm in a cast, a hernia. Sixty-nine years old. First I walked by him, but I had seen him. Strange, I thought —I *know* that guy. That's Gigi. I never called him Daddy cause I never lived with the man. Everybody calls him Gigi because his first name is Eugidio, meaning Eugene—Gigi.

"So all his drinking buddies called him Gigi, and I only knew him by Gigi. I kept staring at him. He kinda looked at me: Who the hell's *this* guy?'

"I said, 'You Gigi, ain't you?"

"He says, 'Ya.'

"I said, 'You know me?'

"He says no.

"I said, 'I'm Eugene. Your son.'

"He said, 'Oh, yeah.'

"It was just like we hadn't seen each other in a couple of days.

"I said, 'You know how long it's been since I seen you? Twenty-one, twenty-two years.'

"He said, 'Yeah, that's right.'

"I said, 'Where you goin'?'

"Oh, just walking around.'

"What happened to your arm?'

"He said, 'Aw, I got in a fuckin' fight.'

"That's what he was, a barroom brawler. Lumps on his head, and the cops, and what-have-you. So we went to a bar. 'Come on,' he says, 'I'll buy you some drinks.' So he took me to this real dive. He introduced me around. I give him fifty bucks. 'Here, keep this in your pocket so you'll have something to drink with if you want to buy yourself and somebody a drink.' Every single person he introduced me to was a derelict of some sort. I said, 'Come on, let's go on down to some of the other haunts.' I had my car. He wanted to walk, which is all he's ever done anyway. He didn't know how to drive a car.

"We went up to Federal Hill, the Italian section of Providence, where he was raised. And all these different joints. *That's your kid?* people said, because he'd never told anybody he had a kid my age. He's had four others from the stepmother, but I'm the only child from his marriage to my mother. So they couldn't believe it. Of course I get a free drink here and there. 'Oh, *you're* the kid? Here, you don't have to buy.' Most of these guys were into booking horses—old businessmen, *mafioso* types, and they humor him. 'Hey, the Great Gigi's got a kid.' The *Great Gigi*. I guess in his younger days he was a pretty tough old cookie. So we hit all these dives and I stayed around Providence for a couple days. I gave him a couple of hundred bucks and I said I'd keep in touch.

"I had to get back and catch a ship. So I got the address of a bar and I wrote a letter or two and he finally wrote me a short letter. I got it downstairs somewhere. So I got his address in Providence, so I'm gonna write him a card from over here. So, that's the end of that. . . .

"Sometimes shipping slows down. Sometimes you slow down. Sometimes I've built up enough unemployment I just feel like laying on the beach and livin' on a hundred twenty-five dollars a week unemployment. I've got my rent paid up for three or four months in advance. My union dues are paid up. I don't have any worries. Just lay there and act like a bum. You tend to run into other bums that way—guys who tell you if you think *you* got troubles, wait'll you hear mine.

"In the merchant marine you're married to the ship. She's your wife. But a lot of marriages are not too romantic. It's a marriage of convenience. I mean—it's been good to me. I reflect back. I worked for a typewriter factory, sold encyclopedias, drove a truck, worked on farms—which I hated with a passion. Insane asylum. Worked in an insane asylum. Worked in a rest home. The army.

"I don't have too much of a future. Those that have no past have a very limited future. I don't have enough brains to do anything else. When I was thirteen, I think it was, they had me down as a mental defective in the orphanage because of running away. They figured I had to be defective mentally because why would I want to run away from a nice orphanage?

"I'm very fatalistic about it. You're born, you live, you die."

Slim and Gut

SLIM AND GUT WENT FORWARD, OVER GREASED CABLES, AROUND loose dunnage, under flatbed trailer trucks—nice work, in the dark, in these seas—to smoke a joint. The ship was starting to roll to heavy swells. Intermittent spray was coming in over the bow. They couldn't smoke in their focscle as they shared quarters with The Ghost. The Ghost was very antidrug. But even if they could smoke dope in their focsles—and some men did—it was not prudent. The smell could linger and get sniffed up by dope dogs; a roach might drop under a bunk and be forgotten; the Captain might walk in; the smell might drift out into the corridor. If a seaman gets busted once he loses his papers, supposedly for good, though not actually. The Coast Guard is less tough on drugs than it pretends to be.

Slim and Gut. Their nicknames fit. Slim was trim and athletic. Gut was round. He ate a lot. They hunched furtively in the winch house trying to get the thing lit. It was hard, with the wind ricocheting around inside the steel chamber. Finally the tip glowed orange. Soon they were giggling. The bow rose on a swell and collapsed into the following trough.

"*Don'* you be rollin' now, ship," said Slim. "You stop that rollin', hear?"

Gut said he wished he were home, he'd never been on a ship this *old.*

"I ain' never been on one o' them new ships," said Slim.

"Ever' ship I get on, they say, 'Maybe we gonna *scrap* this ol' thang.' 'Maybe this gonna be the last trip she make.' 'Maybe she ain' even gonna *make it* to the end o' this trip. Maybe she gonna sink.' "

"Don' be sayin' no such thang,' said Gut.

"Actually, this the best ship I been on," said Slim. "On th'other ships people say, 'Hey messboy, come here.' The Cap'n and officers on this ship, they the first ones I seen look me in the *eye*, man to man. Talk to you not like they talkin' to a messman."

"Yeah, this Cap'n *good.* "

"This the cap'n was on when we made the trip to the Persian Gulf."

"That must be *some* trip. I sorry I miss that one."

"*Miss it?* You ain' miss *nuthin'.* One hunnerd 'n fifteen— when the sun go *down.* "

"*Gracious.* "

"An' you ain' goin' nowhere after you finish workin', 'cause they ain' no place t'go. Uptown they got signs sayin' 'American go home.' An' when those people get down on their knees an' praise Allah, *doan'* you think they ain' lookin' at you at the same time, with one eye."

"You know the worst place I ever been?" said Gut. "Odessa. That's in Russia. I's th'only black man in the whole town. They lookin' at me like I'm from *Mars* or somethin'. They was some black soldiers I ran into. Ethiopians. All the time they askin' me for Donna Summer records. 'Shit,' I say, 'I don' be carryin' no Donna Summer records round the streets with me. Whatcha think, anyhow?' Then they askin' me if I was with the *cause.* ' I say, 'What *cause* you be talkin' 'bout?' They say, the cause 'gainst th'imperialists.' I say, 'What *imperialists* you be talkin' bout?' They say, 'Th' *American* imperialists.' I say, 'What's wrong with America?' They say, 'The black folk in America don' have no freedom.' I tell 'em, 'They better off here?' Shee-yut."

"I been t'Odessa," said Slim. "That ain' no place t'all."

"Well, I tell *you* somethin'. I almos' ended up in Odessa for *good.* Ain' no lie. Nex' mornin' I wake up—it was in this whore-house way the hell outa town, only one'd take black folk—an' I

46

look at my watch. The ship supposed t'sail at seven o'clock. My watch say it almost seven now. *Oh, my Lord Almighty, I'm miles away from the ship and I'm in Russia.*"

"*Gra*cious."

They were standing near a ladder leading down into the number three hold. With no lights on below, the open hatch was a dark hole, out of which came metallic creaking and squeaking.

"This a noisy ship," said Slim.

"This *the* noisiest ship," said Gut.

"Th'ol' man—Charley? Th'AB—th'one look like he dead? He been tellin' me, 'You know that bunk you been sleepin' in? Think o' all your union brothers what *died* in it."

"I don' want t'hear 'bout no such thang, Slim."

"An' he go on about all the *ghosts* they got on these ships. That's why they *creak*, he say, these ol' mothers—that's the *ghost* noise."

"One thang for sure. This ol' bitch got some miles on *her* ass."

A movie was about to be shown in the mess halls. A video cassette player in the officer's mess fed into a TV in the crew's mess twenty yards down a passageway. Pooch, who fixed TVs in his free time at home, was the only one who could make it work right. When he fiddled with the SKEW knob the blizzards on the screen went away.

Bob Cascabel, one of the young ABs, stared into the two banged-up cases of video cassettes. Cascabel was twenty-four years old and from New York. His hair was thick and curly and he had guileless eyes set close together. At two hundred thirty pounds, he was remarkably strong, but he had a gentle manner that gave a kind of moral authority to his physical strength. He read off the choices: "*I Escaped from Devil's Island, The Don Is Dead, Manchu Eagle, Valdez Is Coming, Five on the Black Hand Side*. Usually" he said, "they only give us three kinds of films: Bible films, war films, and fuck films." Pooch did something with the SKEW and everyone slumped back for *I Escaped from Devil's Island*. It was a Forty-second Street version of *Papillon*, with Jim

Brown, nearly naked and covered with Mazola oil, hitting a lot of people and yelling "Shark!" and somehow finding women in the jungle with big bosoms also covered with Mazola oil. Everything was going well, the crew much approving, when the soundtrack unaccountably switched to a Woody Allen movie, *Love and Death*, so that Jim Brown was suddenly slashing French colonial gendarmes with his machete to the sound of Diane Keaton talking about Kierkegaard. Pooch could do nothing to fix it. A number of people stayed anyway, there being little else to do fourteen hundred miles southwest of the Azores.

By now the ship had started to roll and pitch considerably. Sparks came down looking for the Captain with the latest weather report. It said the seas ahead were twenty-five feet and better. That was the good news. Sparks had also been listening to Radio Moscow, and the bad news was the Ayatollah had told Iran to prepare for Holy War with the United States. All Iranian youths were instructed to learn how to shoot and to ride horses.

"God help us," said Sparks.

He finally found the Captain in Chief Engineer Muzzio's cabin where the wide-eyed Chiefy was telling him about a new saltwater leak, in the number two condenser. Chiefy was also convinced there was "a small hole in the hull." The Captain said he was convinced otherwise: "Only small hole we got is in his head, is the way I figure it."

When the movie was over, the Captain went to the mess looking for the Yanson brothers. He had with him a copy of the Articles, the papers all crewmen sign when they come on a ship.

The Yansons were welders, not seamen. They were aboard to install the new sanitary system—one that contained the sewage instead of discharging it directly into the ocean—that would become mandatory on all U.S. ships by January 1, 1980. No one knew when exactly the ship would be back in U.S. waters, but this was November, and if she returned after the new year without the new system, the Coast Guard fine was five thousand dollars a day.

The Yanson brothers were great big redneck lads from Florida. Terry, the younger of the two, was six foot four and built like a tight end. He wore a red polka-dotted cap, chewed Levi

Walker tobacco, and ate enough for three men. On Thanksgiving Day he sent Slim back to the galley four times and still he walked away from the table carrying two pieces of pie and a turkey drumstick. His appetite amazed Slim and Gut. Sometimes they stood next to him while he ate such Brobdingnagian portions and made bets on whether or not he could get through a third steak or a sixth egg or whatever. But what made this gourmandizing truly extraordinary was the concomitant seasickness. Since leaving Charleston, Terry had been ill ninety-seven percent of the time. Neither he nor his older brother, Gary, had ever been to sea before. They had already taken vows never to go again.

Five minutes into the movie tonight, they had both gone to the pantry to throw up. They came back, had another chew of Levi Walker, threw up again, had another chew, threw up. After their fourth visit to the pantry, Gary came back in, looking as though he'd lost a few pints of blood as well as his dinner, lunch, and breakfast, and said it was "about time to pull the plug on this old tub." Just then the Captain arrived with the crew list.

"I don't mean to put it like this," he said, "but I need to know your next of kin."

It was routine. The Articles must include next of kin, just in case; but whatever confidence the Yansons had about making it safely to the other side of the North Atlantic was, after that, diminished.

Mal de Mer

NEXT MORNING, THE MESS WAS A MESS WAS A MESS. BY FIRST light the storm had perked into a full gale. Someone had left a porthole open, and now two inches of cold North Atlantic was sloshing from one end of the pantry to the other. In the middle of the watery devastation stood Yoya, a feral glare in his eyes, ankles awash, but oddly calm, stirring the oceanic soup with a mop, to little effect. Chiefy, at the other end of the mess, was yelling in a hortative frenzy at two oilers who shoveled seawater with dustpans toward the open end of a buzzing, sucking portable pump. The sea had knocked over the garbage can; the silverware tray rammed into the coffee jars, upsetting the sugar container, which upset the cereal boxes, and so on, forever and for aye, ending in a sargasso of cold cuts and condiments, juices and All-Bran. ABs and Ordinary seamen crouched like Indians over spawning salmon, retrieving slices of baloney, teabags, jars of marmalade, spoons, napkins, radishes, coffee grounds, cigarette butts, half-melted salt tablets, globs of chutney.

Slim and Gut were trying to help. Gut, however, had to stay near the big steel sink. He moaned like a dying man. Through the porthole, now tightly shut, he saw the seas rising and falling, their crests turned to spindrift by wind that shrieked through the king posts at forty knots.

Slim, hunched over the sink next to Gut, but in lesser distress

51

kept an anxious eye on his afflicted friend. "Best you go below," he said to Gut. "I take care o' what needs takin' care of."

"Slim," said Gut, "I'd *die* if I went below. I believe I would."

He leaned forward into the sink once more with a dry heave, looking as if he might give up the ghost along with everything else.

A seasick messman is an unlucky man. On the menu this morning was scrambled eggs and brains. And, although the water was eventually pumped out, it left a greasy patina on the ancient linoleum. Walking with trays over that slick surface was tricky, sometimes dangerous.

A few years ago, on one of these midwinter transatlantic passages, a messman carrying a trayful of poached eggs had been thrown fifteen feet by a wave. His head went through a Sheetrock bulkhead. The steward said the man ended up all covered in blood and yolk. "He look like a damn ostrich," he said, "with his haid stuck in there." A wooden board had been screwed over the hole. It was still there.

Mr. Fogarty, the old chief mate, entered by the mess with an inexplicable, bemused look on his face.

The Yansons appeared, faces drawn from having slept no more than ten minutes at a stretch. Someone asked how it was in the hospital where they were quartered. It was barely habitable, but there was simply no other place to put them. Gary stared at the man for a moment, maybe trying to decide if the question was sincere. "Sounded like Walt Disney's fuckin' *horror* house in there," he said. A few hundred pounds of welding rods had come unstrapped and *kawhanged* about all night. Such is the power of seasickness that they did not have the strength to get out of their bunks to lash them down. Anyway, said Gary, they'd probably have been shishkebabed if they'd tried. They weren't anxious to get sliced by the glass plates at the ends of their bunks, either. Terry, who had gone onto the poop deck to throw up—having wearied of staring into the bottom of his wastebasket—slipped on an oil spot, fell on his ass, and had to crawl back to the hospital.

52

The Yansons looked at Slim and Gut leaning into the sinks and laughed. At least others were suffering. Then they ordered mighty helpings of grits, eggs, bacon, toast, juice, coffee, and milk. They were hungry after all they'd been through.

Higgin brought a fresh pot of coffee up to the bridge. He was good at balancing himself on a ship in rough seas, a skill he developed serving on submarines, nuclear and diesel, for seven years. He used to tell horror stories about cruising on the surface through North Atlantic gales while a sub's batteries were being charged. During one storm he was in the forward torpedo room. The sub pitched and lurched and crashed, smelling of diesel fumes, sweat, vomit. Everyone took to carrying little plastic garbage bags, throwing up into them four, five times an hour, gasping for air like drowning men. So this little ol' blow here on the *Columbianna* wasn't much to consider, and walking a pot of coffee up to the bridge without spilling a drop was—a piece of cake.

Higgin had been on the *Grampus* with a messman named Jones, who had had a real talent. He could walk a cup of coffee from the galley up the ladder to the conning tower without spilling a drop. The officers all marveled at this, and said, "Jones, how do you do it?" And Jones would say, "Shucks, guess I was just born with sea legs, or something," and went on carrying cups of coffee without spilling a drop, and even became a minor hero for it, until one day someone discovered Jones's secret. He would take a big gulp of the coffee at the foot of the ladder, hold it while he scrambled up, and just before reaching the top, spit the coffee back into the mug. *Jay-sus,* said Higgin, was the captain in a mood when he found out about that.

Higgin's deep Kentucky voice was inflected with a touch of W. C. Fields. He was a practiced raconteur, and could swear to great effect. His personality fused two utterly dissimilar sensibilities: gentle-born Kentuckian and navy swabbo. He was intelligent, quick-witted, but because he'd never gone to college, had not advanced beyond Chief Petty Officer. That he was only an Able-

Bodied merchant seaman was surprising. But he had stories, especially submarine stories. Of all the things he had done, he was proudest of his submarine days.

He could be sent to jail and fined ten thousand dollars for telling some of these stories. When he mustered out of the navy, he had to sign an oath that made it illegal for him to travel to any Communist country for three years. "Hell," he said, "I ain't even supposed to fly over 'em." (After three years the codes apparently would have changed and his memory would no longer be useful to the KGB.) There was an obvious irony to it all: here he was, a lowly Able-Bodied seaman on a tramp freighter—after eleven years, two months, and twenty-two days in the navy as assistant navigator on several U.S. nuclear submarines. He had done undercover work for the Defense Intelligence Agency in Iran and elsewhere; and he had worked in the Situation Room in Norfolk, where one of the Big Boards is; and knew where the missiles were and where they were pointed—FLASH OVERRIDE stuff. Most of the seven years he had spent on subs was Top Secret stuff. He was allowed to say that he once spent ninety-four days submerged on a mission, but he couldn't say where it was or what they were doing.

One night later in the voyage, on his thirty-first birthday, when the *Columbianna* was coming up the Gulf of Mexico toward Mobile on a balmy evening, a tangerine quarter moon hanging off the stern, Higgin sat on the poop with Bob Cascabel, drinking the last can of beer on board. It was their birthday present to him. Higgin looked up at the moon and said that ten years ago on his birthday he was "at test depth and runnin' like hell."

Yeah? said Cascabel, who by now knew to probe circumspectly. "What ocean were you in?"

"Cain't tell you that," said Higgin, smiling. He had a round face. With his gold-rimmed specs, thinning blond hair, he often looked jolly. It was difficult to imagine that he ever despaired, though he had.

"Well, what's '*test depth*'?" Cascabel persisted.

54

"Cain't tell you that, neither."

"Well, what do you mean, 'Runnin' like hell'?"

Higgin smiled and said nothing. The *ta-dum ta-dum ta-dum* rumble of the screw vibrated up through their shinbones.

Another time, everyone was talking excitedly about the new movie, *Apocalypse Now,* when Higgin fell noticeably silent.

"I think *Heart of Darkness* was better," said Bob Cascabel. Cascabel knew literature and knife fighting equally well. "I like Conrad."

"You know," said one of the younger Ordinaries, "that guy Conrad stole that story *word for word* from the movie?"

Bob Cascabel sighed and said that he had not known that. The Ordinary asked Higgin if he'd seen the movie. He shook his head.

"Aw, it's some film, man. You gotta go see it."

"I knew some of those poor bastards—what they went through. I know I couldn't see it."

A few nights later, during watch on the starboard wing deck, he told a story. It wasn't top secret; or if it was, it didn't matter anymore.

He had been Chief Petty Officer assigned to a surface ship in Vietnam. Two days earlier they'd dropped a navy SEAL team off near Cua Tung. SEAL is Sea Air and Land—the navy's version of the Green Berets. The SEAL team had orders to bring back a Vietcong cadre as hostage. The morning of the second day, at the appointed hour, Higgin and a few men went ashore in a large rubber landing craft to pick up the SEAL team. Halfway to shore, they heard gunfire coming from the jungle beyond the beach. The first SEAL broke through the jungle cover, pushing a prisoner in front of him. The second SEAL appeared, also with a prisoner. Soon all nine of them were on the beach, each with a prisoner. The SEALs began to run toward the landing raft. And as they ran, they killed the prisoners, one by one. They didn't shoot them. They knifed them, or snapped their necks. By the time they reached Higgin's raft, only one prisoner was still alive. Higgin got the SEALs back, under fire, to the ship. Its captain, who had

55

been watching the whole thing, approached the commander of the SEAL team and demanded to know why they'd killed so many men. The SEAL gazed at him, paused, and then, with a look in his eyes Higgin could not convey, said, "My orders were to bring back *one* hostage."

"Their training," said Higgin. "It's their training." He fell quiet and said nothing for the remainder of the watch.

Higgin

When he was fourteen, Higgin wrote a poem called "God-damn This World."

> *Goddamn this world and all that sin.*
> *I hate these people with their religious hymns.*
> *I hate the world when it moans and cries*
> *Over people who've long since died.*
>
> *Goddamn, Goddamn, Goddamn this world*
> *With all of its hate I see so well.*
> *We shall die with all the rest,*
> *Liquor and fire will put us to our death.*

Higgin was born into a blue-blood, green money Kentucky family. A great-greatuncle had started one of the largest distilleries in the United States. Another uncle founded one of the largest tobacco companies. His grandfather raised horses. Higgin himself owned half interest in a coal mine, which earned him a great deal more than his Able-Bodied seaman's base wage of thirty-two dollars and change a day. He was a smart, hard-drinking, well-traveled young man who could talk knowledgeably about proxy battles, shotgunning, bird dogs, equilibrium polygons, nuclear war, and the best way to cook a dove. He knew by heart long stretches of Shakespeare, Tennyson, Thomas Gray. Unlike everyone else aboard, he did not have to be out here. He wanted to be out here.

When he was sixteen, he lost his five best friends: one in a car that went off the road, one to an accidental shotgun blast; another was stabbed at a dance and two died of natural causes. That same year his favorite uncle was killed by his son-in-law in a hunting accident. And then Higgin's brother put a pistol to his head and killed himself.

"It makes you cold," said Higgin. "It made me real cold at that point in my life."

He raised hell at various military schools and ended up in the navy. He went to Vietnam, Iran, Italy, London. The big moment in his navy career came on September 20, 1977, somewhere between Naples and Tunis, when the nuclear submarine he was guiding through the Mediterranean slammed into an undersea mountain and nearly sank. He could remember the day in total detail, starting with the orders he was giving to the helmsman of the U.S.S. *Ray* at the time of the accident:

" *'Full dive on the fair water planes. Gimme a fifteen degree down bubble. Passing two hundred feet.'*

'Passing two hundred feet, aye.'

'Passing three hundred feet.'

'Passing three hundred feet, aye.'

'Zero bubble.'

'Zero bubble, aye.'

'Take charge of your planes. Passing four hundred feet. Coming to four hundred ten feet.'

'Four hundred feet, aye.'

"She hit at four hundred and ten feet.

"When we grounded, everyone was knocked over. The Diving Officer of the Watch was thrown into the controls. The Chief of the Watch was thrown into the controls as well.

"I thought that we'd hit another submarine. There was an operation we were headed for, a NATO type of operation. We were doin' about sixteen knots [almost eighteen miles per hour], and I—I hit the deck. Everyone else hit the deck. Charts, pencils, dividers, everything was just *bang*—it went from sixteen knots to full stop.

"I picked myself up and looked over at the Chief of the Watch. He was pullin' his teeth outa the ballast control panel, and I looked at him and I thought for sure that we'd hit another submarine—one of ours, one that we knew was there—and that it was my fault, that I hadn't plotted correctly. And I thought, *The poor sons of bitches.*

"I said, 'Emergency Blow!' The Chief of the Watch—he was one of the men who worked for me, and he was first-class— grabbed the chicken switch. That's what Emergency Blow is called, where you dump all your air flask into the ballast tanks. He held the switch and looked over at the Officer of the Deck. The Officer of the Deck had broken his ankle in a basketball game about four weeks prior. Because his foot was exposed, he broke three toes when we grounded. He had a pained expression. He was a hurt frog. He couldn't quite say it yet. I told the guy 'Emergency Blow!' and I was heading toward the ballast control panel to take it and blow it myself, get us to the surface, to find out, you know—pick up any survivors. The Officer of the Deck finally spat out 'Emergency Blow.' My compatriot threw the chicken switch and up we went. It was a controlled ascent. It was level all the way.

"But it was slow, cause our center of gravity was thrown forward and out of the equilibrium polygon, which is—never mind. We were sinking on the starboard side. The Officer of the Deck raised the periscope to check for dark shadows. There was land nearby. We deduced our position by visual means, and found we were right over the top of a seamount that we thought we'd cleared. It was a pinnacle, like what you'd find in Nevada, those things that rise up out of the desert. I'd quit smokin' for eight months, and I asked for a cigarette.

"Once I found out that actually we'd hit a pinnacle, I sent one of my men, who was hurt pretty bad, below to be stitched, and I took the watch. The Captain sent a message to the commander of Submarine Flotilla Eight, an' he had tears in his eyes, knowin' that his career was ruined, an'—God—I envied the man. He maintained his equanimity well. He's a good man. He briefed his crew on what happened. He was able to send the message—

communication gear was still workin'. And they sent a message back sayin' they had an escort en route.

"Dickson was hurt, suspected broken neck, skull cut up pretty bad. Others . . .

"I guess about seven hours after the accident I went below an' crawled inta my cabin, an' I just laid there and looked at th' overhead and thought of all the implications. The operation we were goin' to was ruined, the Captain's career was over. I just laid down there, an' I remember bein' asked several questions by the officers. I don't remember what I said. I thought it was coherent, but I found later that it wasn't, and that I musta been in a severe case of shock. I never slept, just laid there.

"Finally I got up a couple hours later, went up and stayed in the control until we moored. And the funny part of it was that comin' into the harbor—it was about two or three o'clock in the mornin'—it's tricky, cause you're goin' through rocks, great, big fuckin' *rocks,* rocks that long. And we went through in the middle of a rainstorm, heavy rainstorm, which I thought was sort of a plus for our navigational skill.

"We got into port. I called up my daddy. He was in the hospital for a minor overhaul and repairs. He'd been up late at night, as was his habit, readin', and he heard it over the radio that the *Ray* had grounded in the Med. He knew that I was assistant navigator on it. He cried, because he thought, you know, that I was gone too. He'd already lost one son. But he was okay once I called him."

At the end of a lengthy investigation, Higgin was officially exonerated, but was given something called a "nonpunitive letter of caution," which he said was "just a personal letter from the Admiral to me sayin', 'You better do better next time.' " The inquiry determined that the accident resulted from a conspiracy of small details—highly technical and classified—and that no one person was responsible.

Assigned to duty in Norfolk, Higgin and a friend started to go on nightly drinking binges. In the morning, they would go to the navy hospital, where his friend's girl friend was chief nurse, to get oxygen and half-hour intravenous feedings of plasma to alleviate their hangovers. Then they'd report to work. Not long afterward Higgin mustered out of the navy.

Though his navy training had given him skills far more sophisticated than those of any master of a simple merchant ship, the Coast Guard would not allow him to count any of his navy sea time toward a merchant marine officer's license, because it was *underwater* sea time. So here he was—after hundreds of thousands of dollars of training, one war, and dozens of cold war missions, having guided billion-dollar war machines through tight places (give or take a few seamounts), secrets of the Big Board locked in his memory, accumulating sea time on the *Columbianna*, dripping paint and standing watch, so he could sit for his third mate's license examination.

He was a gleeful misanthrope, Higgin. There was a little routine he used to do, some Strother Martin lines. Strother Martin, who played the warden in *Cool Hand Luke*, was Higgin's favorite actor. Late at night in the focsle and full of rum, Higgin would boom out in Strother's ornery accents:

"Shanghai McCoy's the name. *Been* everwhere. *Done* everthin'. Been round the Horn, sailed the Seven Seas. Been all *over* the world, and that's how come I know people is just . . . *so* . . . *mis-er-a-ble.*"

But in sentimental moods, he used to recite a poem he'd heard a hundred ports ago.

> *When ships are no more than ships to me,*
> *And there's no place left as I'd like to see;*
> *When fun's all flat, and jokes all stale,*
> *There's no taste left in the cakes and ale,*
> *Stitch me up as soon as you like,*
> *In a corner of worn out sail;*
> *With oily stones at my heels and head,*
> *Toss me overboard, and I'll be dead.*

Mr. Dexter

LATE THAT NIGHT, IN THE DARK, THE CAPTAIN AND ONE OF THE Third Mates poured themselves some of Higgin's coffee, managing not to spill any. They talked about the rpms, the squall line coming down from the north, the period of roll. The Captain was careful never to appear too concerned while Mr. Dexter had the watch. Mr. Dexter, at sixty-seven, had more time at sea than any other man aboard. He knew everything about the sea. He was a third mate because he was content to be a third mate, and wanted neither the headaches nor the salary of higher rank. He needed no advice, and the Captain respected that, even if it made him feel a bit useless on the bridge. They liked each other, and got along well.

The Captain went onto the wing to make sure Butts, the Ordinary lookout, was sober. Butts had just relieved Pooch, ten minutes late as usual. Tonight Pooch decided not to say anything about it; he just furrowed his eyebrows, sighed, and swallowed another Tagamet—his punctured intestines were bothering him.

Back on the bridge, Mr. Dexter stood over the radar, circling squalls with his grease pencil. The radar bathed his face in soft bluish light. His hair was thick and gray, the corners of his eyes were creased from five decades of squinting into sun and wind, but his face, though weathered, retained a native kindness, even in the unnatural light. The Captain returned and stood next to Mr. Dexter hoping, so it seemed, that he might need help.

"Well," he said, fishing, "suppose everthin's okay, I guess."

"Oh sure," said Mr. Dexter, not looking up. "Expect she'll have blown over by sunrise."

"Well, you know where I am if you need me."

"That's right," said Mr. Dexter, circling another squall.

"Well, good night, Tom."

"Good night, Captain." The Captain disappeared into the chart room. The open door threw a quick slice of harsh light into the bridge, then shut.

Not long afterward, a big broaching wave lifted the ship onto its crest. She hovered there for a long second, then slid sideways into the trough, rolling forty-five degrees. Butts, the lookout, was clinging to the rail of the wing deck.

"During the day's one thing," said Butts, facing into the wind, which blew his beard back onto his neck. "I don't mind when it's rough during the day. I can see the waves during the day. I don't like it when I can't see 'em. And it's cold. I don't like that, neither."

Seven days out of Charleston, Butts was just starting to dry out. He was twenty-four but looked ten years older. He was going bald, had a long, stringy blond beard, and his eyes were empty, showing only the strain of too much drinking. He had already been in and out of the Public Health's alcoholic ward a few times. When Butts was seventeen a judge had given him the choice of three careers: jail, school, or the merchant marine. The Vietnam war was on then, and men were needed for Military Sealift Command ships. After the war, Butts stayed on, used to the life and the good money. He lived in Norfolk and spent his time at a bar owned by a man named Gus. Butts said he wished he were there right now, getting drunk.

Mr. Dexter was twisting the CLUTTER knob on the radar set, trying to focus out the squalls. Someone asked him if he'd ever been to Snug Harbor, the home for old seamen.

Mr. Dexter laughed. "No," he said. "I don't want to go to the Snug Harbor."

The *Columbianna* took a wave broadside, righting herself sluggishly.

"They got a window there, from the old church," Mr. Dexter was told, "with an inscription that says, 'Be of good cheer, for there shall be no loss of life among ye, but only of the ship.'"

Mr. Dexter said he liked that. He was a Catholic, kept a phial of holy water in his cabin. It was from the shrine of Saint Jude in New Orleans. When Mr. Dexter was young and the ships he was on came to New Orleans, he went on drinking bouts—three to four days of hard going—and always ended up at that shrine, in the little grotto chapel where candles burned and holy water dripped softly from a crease in the rock. In the cool and semidark he felt welcome, although he was without money, unshaven, and sapped.

Mr. Dexter was not an unhappy man. On the contrary: he gave off a nourishing cheer. He was a respected seaman. The rumors said he was rich, exceedingly rich, that he had bought a lot of gold when it at a hundred twenty dollars an ounce, and didn't have to be out here at all, a sixty-seven-year-old third mate on a North Atlantic winter tramp run to—Lord—Bremerhaven. The truth was he had done well with gold, though he was not the Croesus the rumors made him out to be. Still, he did not have to be out here; he could have retired a long time ago. But he was not a stationary man. Even when he was between ships he couldn't stay put. After a few days staring at his never-used lawn mower, he would invite a few friends over, mix everyone six or seven martinis and, when they were good and bombed, suggest they all jump in the car and drive to JFK airport. Then they'd catch a flight somewhere.

Where?

"Oh, anywhere. I went to London quite frequently. Los Angeles, went to Los Angeles fairly often. Never get tight with me, I used to say. You never knew where you'd wake up the next morning, but there was a good chance it wouldn't be Port Jervis."

He had never married. A maiden sister who had lived with him had died of cancer the year before. Now he kept the house, but he really lived on freighters, preferring tramps because they took him to unexpected destinations. It did not matter where he went: it was the going that kept him alive.

65

He had run away from home at thirteen, after feeding all his schoolbooks to the landlady's goats. He grew up in what is now Spanish Harlem in New York City. He had scattered his seed all over the world but had never come back for the harvest.

As a cadet, he had sailed on the *Joseph Conrad*, the sailing ship now berthed permanently at Mystic Seaport Museum. He had sailed through three wars, took out a man's appendix during a submarine attack, got drunk with Hemingway in Paris, fought a whale. He'd seen a man commit suicide with lint.

"This messman," the story went, "had gone a little berserk and attacked the purser. They got him down to his cabin—and it's quite a struggle with those psychos, they're strong—and got him manacled into his bed, and handcuffed and all the rest. Two days went by and the purser comes running up and says there's no movement under his blanket. He'd covered himself up with the wool blanket. So we go down, and, oh, the purser wasn't about to get *near* him. This fellow had already bitten him once. I pulled back the blanket and there *was* no movement. His face was pale and blue and there weren't any vital signs, no breath on the mirror. Well, we couldn't figure out how he died—weren't any doctors on board or anything. I looked up his nose and down his throat to see if I could find any blood, and they were all clogged up with little woolen balls, balls of wool he'd scraped off the blanket and put up his nose and down his throat. They must have gotten into his lungs and killed him. He killed himself like that."

Mr. Dexter had lots of scars. One day on the bridge he and Sparks were overheard swapping stories about their bleeding ulcers, dentures, bum knees, hernias, tickers (Mr. Dexter's heart had stopped once on the operating table), knife punctures, crushed toes, gassed lungs, scorched corneas, clap, torpedo concussions. Yet here he was, in Arnold Lunn's phrase, unkilled for so long.

If the moon came out from behind a cloud and threw light on the water a certain way, it would remind Mr. Dexter of something. One night off Brittany, after a thunderstorm, he got very excited telling the story:

"This was during the war, off the Great Barrier Reef, on a troop transport. We had this message from the navy that a Jap sub had gotten through the lines and was in our area looking for us. We had a brigade of crack soldiers we were delivering to the Aleutian Islands. Special Forces. This Jap sub knew all about it, oh, and they were certainly looking for us. The Old Man had been up on the bridge forty hours straight, no coffee break or anything, and, well, our nerves were shot for sure by this time.

"I took the watch. And the moon came out behind some clouds—like tonight—and ahead of us I see this . . . *thing* on the horizon. I think—*the Jap sub!* I sound the GQ [General Quarters]. I'm going to ram that Jap son of a bitch. I'm calling down to the engine room and telling them to give me everything they've got—fifteen nozzles! I say, 'Get ready to ram. We're going to ram that Jap bastard.' The engineer says, *'What?'* I say, 'We're going to ram that Jap submarine.' The guy in charge of the navy gunners calls me up on the bridge and says 'What's going *on* here?' I say, 'We're going to ram this sub. Get on the guns!'

"But the guns turn out to be jammed from salt water. They can't get the triggers to depress. Fine time to find out. 'Well, to hell with the guns,' I say. 'Get ready to ram. Get ready!' We're almost on top of it. *'Stand fast!'* People are running all over the ship. There's all sorts of confusion. Now we're about thirty yards from it, closing fast, about to hit—and up out of the water comes a big tail. Never *seen* such a sight, water running off the flukes in the moonlight. He must have been asleep, the old boy.

"I turn around and the Captain's there, behind me, shaking his head. He says, 'It's a whale, Mate.' 'Yeah,' I say, 'I guess so.' Would've rammed him if he hadn't sounded. But I can never forget the way the moonlight looked on his tail."

Mr. Dexter took his glasses off and rubbed the bridge of his nose.

Sometimes, when he talked about the war, he had an unconscious way of juxtaposing the horrible and the quaint: the crew of a torpedoed tanker burning to death in a flaming lake of ignited oil and his dog, watching it from the deck of the ship, wagging its tail at the curious sight. Mr. Dexter also had a cat during the war, a midget cat that hated everyone—"even me"—and once curled up in a spot beneath a porthole, warm, content, as though it knew it was protected by the flanking corvettes that escorted the freighter through the icy, sub-infested waters off Murmansk.

Unlike the Captain, Mr. Dexter cared greatly what cargoes were aboard—the hotter the better. He was pleased to be carrying tanks and "sensitive weapons." At the start of the voyage he went through the cargo manifest to see what kind of weapons they were but found nothing more specific.

"They don't like it to get out we got hot cargo aboard," Mr. Dexter had said.

"You mean we're carrying *nuclear* cargo?" he was asked.

"No. Well, they say no, but we got our own ideas about that. I was on one once." He laughed. *"Boy, was that a hot bastard."*

That night in Charleston when the Moslems took over the Grand Mosque, Mr. Dexter was enormously buoyed by the news that the *Kitty Hawk* and the *Midway* were en route to the Gulf.

"Oh Jeez," he'd told the Captain. "Here we go."

"Whaddya mean, *'Here we go'?"* said the Captain, ears going up like a jackrabbit's.

"We'll probably be attached to the fleet now. She's built for invasions, you know."

"Well, I ain't heard *nothin* about no invasion."

"You think they're going to send you a registered letter?"

Mr. Dexter and the old chief mate, Mr. Fogarty, were always trying to convince the Captain that death was not only inevitable, but imminent.

This night of the storm, after the Captain had left the bridge feeling a bit unwanted, Mr. Dexter seemed to be at the end of his tether. He said he was looking for something. He was looking to go out with a bang.

"I don't care about the blaze of glory or any of that," he said once, leaning on the rim of the wing deck, staring at the roiling ocean. "I just don't want to die from the cancer—take a year dying in the hospital, like Ed Richmond or Charley Duke. That's no way to go." He shrugged. "This run here, it's a fucking pain in the ass. But I wanted this old girl. I heard she was in port and I signed on because I thought, well, with all this business going on over there, she'd be headed into the Med and then maybe to the Gulf to join the fleet." He smiled. "That way, see, I could go out fast."

Shortly afterward, at ten minutes to midnight, the twelve-to-four watch turned to on the bridge. It was Mr. Darby's watch. He was the other third mate, and the only academy-trained officer aboard. The others had all come up through the hawsepipe, as the expression goes (the hawsepipe is the hole in the bow through which the anchor chain passes). This was only the second ship he had been on since graduating from the Massachusetts Maritime Academy. He was obviously nervous and ill at ease, and had a twitch in both eyes that he said was from uncomfortable contact lenses, but wasn't. At twenty-two he still had a peach-fuzzy chin. His hair was blond, and he was a bit plump. Mr. Dexter spent extra time—the courtesy of an older sea officer toward a younger peer—acquainting him with the position, seas, wind, speed, course, loran fixes, and rpms. Mr. Darby nodded silently to all of it.

Mr. Dexter asked him how it was below. Mr. Darby said he had seen the Captain, who was muttering about the Chief Engineer, how he was going to "cashier his ass" first chance he got. Chiefy was agitating about the number two condenser and wanted to put into the Azores for repairs. He did not admit it to Mr. Dexter, but the prospect of pulling into the Azores worried Mr. Darby, because he had with him something he was not supposed to have, even though he had his reasons for having it.

Cain and Able

As a freshly commissioned third mate, Mr. Darby had gotten a billet on his first ship without delay. He arrived at the dock in Norfolk, his heart pounding, filled with the happy presentiments of a young officer going to sea for the first time. But when he reached the end of the dock and saw his ship, his heart really began to pound. How had this rotten old heap kept afloat so long? Did she actually traverse the North Atlantic—and _regularly?_ Had it not been for the stevedores on her decks or the smoke issuing from her stack, he would have supposed she was on her way to be broken up. He looked at his shipping card, checked the name written there against the name on the bow. The two were, incredibly, identical. She was the _Samarra,_ and hauled coal between Norfolk and Rotterdam. That same night Mr. Darby left for Holland on the first of three _Samarra_ trips.

Several days out, the captain mustered all hands on the poop deck for an unusual occasion. An old sailor had died a week earlier. His last wish was that his ashes be scattered from the stern of the first ship he had sailed on, the _Samarra._ The captain had prepared a solemn ceremony, including the playing of taps on a cassette tape recorder. The men assembled, the purser hit the PLAY button, and the air was filled with a tinny but recognizable taps. The ashes were in a plastic jar. The captain unscrewed the lid, held the jar in one hand, and began to read the service. The ship rolled gently, but the men stood firm, and when the captain came to the line, "We now commit his body to the sea," he poured the ashes over the stern. But as he poured, the updraft caused by the ship's forward motion blew back into his face, carrying with it most of the departed's last mortal remains, which settled down the front of the captain's uniform. At this the captain, who suffered from allergies, started sneezing. Faced with a situation of diminishing punctilio, he insisted on reading the funeral rite through to the end.

"The Lord bless thee and—*ah-ahchoooo!*—keep thee. The Lord make his f-f-face to sh-*achoo!*-shine upon thee. . . ."

The crew found it hard to maintain a posture of bereavement, and their laughter put the captain into a snit for the remainder of Mr. Darby's first voyage.

On Mr. Darby's second trip to Rotterdam, the bosun, a grizzled old diabetic who drank incessantly, died in his sleep. They put him in the meat locker and cabled for instructions from the next of kin on how to dispose of the body. After several days a cable came back from a cousin who had not seen the bosun in thirty years; he didn't really care *what* they did with the body.

So they sewed the bosun up in canvas, put the traditional last stitch through the nose, and put him over the side, with taps and without incident.

It was the third trip on the *Samarra* that had caused, indirectly, Mr. Darby's present difficulty. One of the Able-Bodied seamen aboard was named Ferguson. Able he was not. Although an AB is supposed to be skilled at the wheel, Ferguson was unfamiliar with helmsmanship. The captain asked Mr. Darby to teach him how to steer. But Ferguson was not agreeable to the idea, not at all. The first morning of instruction, he suddenly swung the helm hard over to port. Just as everyone had picked himself off the deck, Ferguson swung the wheel hard over to starboard. The captain, down below in his cabin, shaving, fell forward into the mirror and sank his straight razor into his chin. He stormed up to the bridge, blue—and red—in the face, screaming, and found Ferguson doing zigzags, blithe as a kid at a carnival, and Mr. Darby entreating him to stop.

Had the ship not been undermanned, the captain would

72

have put Ferguson in irons and on bread and water (it is still, though seldom, done these days); instead he yelled at him for a good five minutes, then went back to his cabin to bandage his chin, which had been dripping onto the bridge throughout the harangue.

Ferguson changed after that. He began to wear only his underpants, and fashioned himself a makeshift spear by tying a sharp paint scraper to the end of a six-foot pole. He carried it with him everywhere—to meals, to work, to bed. His eyes became weird. Some mental fever was in him. At night he climbed the rigging, stood atop the mast, and keened at the moon, shouting, said Mr. Darby, all kinds of crazy things.

What things?

"Oh, how he was Blackbeard and the ship was doomed."

One day they saw him walking on the gunwales, doing a sort of tightrope act between the deck and the Atlantic Ocean, using his spear as a balancing pole.

Sent forward to relieve the bow lookout, he would creep up stealthily, position his mouth a foot from the lookout's ear, and scream, "HERE I AM!"—nearly inducing myocardial infarction in the lookout, absorbed as he was in reverie after two hours of silent watching.

By then Ferguson had become a real problem. The crew was complaining. No one wanted to be speared or to wrestle Ferguson into handcuffs. He was a big man, and strong. Nevertheless, the captain was still determined that Ferguson learn how to steer and that Mr. Darby teach him. Mr. Darby was understandably reluctant, but he obeyed.

One night Ferguson started doing the zigzags again. Mr. Darby said to him, "Ferguson, I'm tired of this. Put it on auto and go get a cup of coffee."

Ferguson said very quietly, "Thank you, Mate," as though he had proved his point and finally won. And that was the last Mr. Darby or anyone saw of Ferguson.

Next morning he did not turn to for his watch. In his cabin the crew found a length of manila line, knotted at two-foot intervals like a climbing rope, fastened to a bunk and leading out the open porthole. They searched the ship, but he was not aboard. The captain calculated where the ship was when Ferguson had last been seen, eight hours before, and turned the *Samarra* around, retracing the course. The crew threw life jackets and pieces of buoyant dunnage over the side every half hour in a futile but earnest attempt to preserve the life of a man who by now had probably succeeded in taking his own. When she reached the approximate spot where he'd last been seen, the *Samarra* turned around and set her course again for Rotterdam, still half an ocean away.

Mr. Darby signed off after that trip and stayed ashore longer than he would have ordinarily before catching his next ship, the *Columbianna*. After flying into Norfolk, where he would sign aboard, he stopped at a pawnshop. He paid sixty dollars for a .32 caliber Saturday Night Special, now concealed in his cabin. Seamen on U.S. merchant ships are not permitted even sheath knives, because they can be drawn too quickly; and only the captain is permitted a gun. If a customs agent in the Azores were to stumble onto Mr. Darby's .32, he could be thrown in jail and would forfeit his mate's license. Four years of the academy wasted. Still, Mr. Darby was reluctant to heave the gun over the side. It wasn't the sixty dollars; it was the crew that worried him.

Jefferson worried him. Jefferson was a black oiler from Mobile, twenty-two years old. He had scars all over his face, put there by knives, razors, chains, fists. He was not an easygoing fellow, Jefferson. He had a mean aura. Whenever he wasn't working, he smoked dope, said it "mellowed" him out. In fact it did not mellow him out. When he smoked, his eyes narrowed to a minatory stare, and he would talk about how good he was with a knife or a gun or a baseball bat, or whatever.

Sometimes dope induced in him a nostalgic mood, and he would talk fondly about his first zip gun, or the first old woman he'd robbed and beaten, the best jail he'd been in, the worst. He had once lost his seaman's papers for sixteen months for attacking a second engineer. (By the time he signed off the *Columbianna*, amid strained circumstances, he had threatened to kill roughly

74

one third of the crew, as well as the company's insurance investigator.) Almost everyone went out of his way to be civil to Jefferson, because he had a reputation. Three years ago he had shot his brother to death with a .357 Magnum.

The merchant seaman's world is small. Jefferson was known in the maritime brotherhood as the Man Who Killed His Brother. Certainly, no one aboard was inclined to bring up the subject with him. He only talked about it once, with the Chief Electrician, a black man named Francis, on a night when the two of them got drunk in Bremerhaven. Francis told everyone *never* to mention it to Jefferson, that it would be a very poor idea.

Francis said, "It was, uh, self-defense."

"Self-defense?"

"His brother was having some problems. He was having a change of life, like."

One night after watch, Jefferson invited one of the new ordinaries into his cabin for a midnight smoke. He had sealed his door with putty so the smoke wouldn't leak out into the passageway, and had installed what he called a "Captain lock," an inside bolt that guaranteed privacy. After four joints, Jefferson was mellow and explaining how he'd caught the Second Engineer in the Adam's apple with a pipe wrench. He said the guy had it coming to him, he'd been complaining to the Captain about Jefferson's attitude. He stared at the ordinary through slitted eyelids and said, "I got to be a man till the day I die."

The ordinary was foggy with smoke. "Got any brothers or sisters?" he asked. As soon as he said it, he wished he hadn't.

Jefferson said nothing, did not look up from the joint he was rolling. After a silent minute, he reached into a shelf behind him and brought out a photo album.

The ordinary opened it to the first page. There was a color photograph of a young man, wearing a tuxedo with ruffled shirt, laid out in an open coffin. Jefferson's eyes bored into the ordinary.

"This is your—"

"My brother."

"What happened?"

There was a long pause, during which Jefferson's eyes never left his.

"Accident."

The Second Mate worried Mr. Darby.

The Second was an awkward, taciturn man named Burke. He had not a friend on the ship. He took his rank seriously, bullied those beneath him and hated those above him, especially the Captain. In the Captain's presence, he was obliging, correct, obsequious; at other times, his resentment wriggled into the open like a snake from beneath an overturned rock. He was a sad, lonely, bitter man, who made frequent pathetic remonstrations about minor issues. The Captain once left the bridge, having said of the weather, "It's every bit of Seven." Burke, hands clasped behind him, pacing back and forth, said to Bob Cascabel, who had the helm, "Well, if the Captain says it is Force Seven, then Force Seven it is. He is, after all, the Captain. Far be it from *me* to dispute what the Captain says. He is a man of some . . . experience, I suppose we must call it. . . ." Cascabel thought, *Deliver me from assholes.*

When Mr. Darby once arrived on the bridge five minutes early to relieve Burke for his meal break, Burke turned on him, and with palpable hatred in his voice, said, "I don't want to jeopardize your employment with this company, so I suggest you go down to your cabin and read your contract. *Then come up here and relieve me at seventeen hundred hours!*" With that, he huffed out onto the wing deck.

Burke's face was misshapen, the result perhaps of having gone through a windshield or having been severely burned. Great skill, the crew supposed, had gone into its reconstruction. Still, the right eye, exophthalmic, rested too high, the eyebrow slashing down above it like an *accent grave*. The skin was reddish and pitted. The face had an ineluctably malevolent aspect. His smile, if it came, seemed a contortion, as though muscle, trigeminus, and bone had lost their congenital ability to coordinate. Slim called him "the Evil Eye," and one day, making idle talk in the mess, Gut was overheard to say of him, "I hope he not be born that way, else he be a monster to 'is momma."

The Ghost worried Mr. Darby—in a different way. It was mostly during Mr. Darby's watch that the Ghost would go forward, often in moderately rough seas, to perch on the bow and converse with King Neptune. It was therefore Mr. Darby's responsibility to make sure he did not fall into the ocean.

Chief Engineer Muzzio worried him. Chiefy once came careening up to the bridge, an especially crazed look on his face, after he received a note from the Captain asking him to apply fifteen nozzles of steam to the turbine blades for better speed. (Nozzles were a constant problem between Chiefy and the Captain.) Looking like a hobgoblin on a fistful of bennies, Chiefy swore and yelled and told Mr. Darby to tell the Captain that if he wanted fifteen nozzles of steam, when thirteen was what any rational man would ask for, then he could go fuck himself. Mr. Darby twitched and offered politely to, er, bring up the matter of the two extra nozzles with the Captain just as soon as he could, and Chiefy stormed off the bridge.

Then there was Rocco. He was twenty-two, from Brooklyn, with arms like firewood and eyes that begged, through all the boasting, for sympathy, for something other than what he'd gotten all his life.

Rocco had been trained in the SEAL. "Took four shrinks to make me whole," said Rocco.

The general consensus aboard was that eight would have been better. On the other hand no one was really sure Rocco had actually been with the SEAL in Vietnam—he would have been very young. Or that he did occasional guerrilla jobs for the Anastasio mob, as he said; or that *anything* he said was true, even though he was clearly a violent young man. Within a month he would be chewing Valiums, punching steel bulkheads until his knuckles bled, screaming with nightmares, reading from the Book

77

of Revelation—the juicy parts, as he called them—and talking about how it was all going to end in a rain of fire and blood.

Rocco came up the bridge one afternoon to change the lightbulbs. He'd been reading the Book of Revelation and had that unsettling grin, and as he worked he told Mr. Darby how it was going to be, "A rain of blood and fire, man, and people gettin' cut, like in *two*—and up to their *necks* in blood."

Rocco worried him.

Rocco

PEOPLE USED TO SAY OF ROCCO THAT EVERYTIME HE STARTED
talking about something it ended with somebody getting machine-gunned. If he talked about _bluebirds_ somebody would get
machine-gunned. He always told stories about his adventures in
Vietnam with the SEALs, even though no one believed him. He
would swing any conversation around to how many Viet Cong he
had killed with his bare hands, how the M-14 beat the M-16 any
day, how . . . it all amounted to twenty-five SEAL missions.
However true that was, Rocco did say his navy career ended in
the brig. Soon afterward, he joined the merchant marine:

"The reason why I'm out here is to get away from land—
people. It's not because I hate them or nothing like that—but
land's just too crowded, everybody gets on your nerves too much
around there. The reason why I come out here is everybody's at
peace out here. You know, I just go where I please, sit on the bow,
sit peacefully. That's how I feel about it.

"I lost my temper this morning. Somebody come up to me
—you know once in a while I get up kinda late, a few minutes
after eight o'clock, okay? It was—I won't mention no names cause
I don't wanna get in trouble. I say, 'Hey, man, what're you gettin'
on my throat for?' And this other guy comes by and he was in a
bad mood too and he pushed my ass and _bam!_ How the hell are
you? And I got mad and kicked the ice machine and when I was
on the fantail I started beating the hell out of the oil drums

because it makes me feel better, gets it out of me. 'Cause if I hang around the same area where people are around I'll pick on them. That's when I start using them as basketballs. And I mean what I say, I start throwing them around.

"The thing why I cry is because of my temper. A real hot temper, I really got it. I cry real hard. I wanna get it out of me before I hurt somebody. I'm not saying I'm really gonna hurt somebody. Like I don't fight to *hurt* somebody, like break their arms—just to get 'em just to stay away from me, you know: keep your clearance. But if you keep comin' at me I'll just keep punching you down. That's how I am. I don't like to jump on people and beat 'em up. That's not me.

"I could be a true friend. See, I'm the type of person I could be a true friend to another true good person. Have a long life friendship. These days—man—these days been so miserable you can't even find a woman that wants to stay with you for four months married. You still get divorced. I don't know if it's just getting bad. Like I'm just protecting myself against the world. I know the world's gonna try to involve me and I'm not gonna let 'em. This world's just getting bad.

"Well, I think I'm going to be living in an age, a very evil age. If you look in the older days there wasn't as much as evil as we're having right now. Year by year it's getting even more evil than any other. The old days there wasn't that much fornication as we're havin' now. Now it's just all free enterprise.

"*Yeah*, it's gonna get worse. It's gonna get *a lot* worse. I hate to think negatively like that but that's the way it's gonna happen. That's the way it's made to happen.

"I believe in the Bible very much. The King James version, that's the best one. I understand 'thees and thous' better than the new ones. The British language, it's all right. It's got real meaning to it. It's got a meaning that just wants to tear you out of your seat.

"See, the way I think—you know, the one thing I fear—I know somewhere in my life, somewhere God's gonna pull me out of where I am now and is gonna use me for his tool, like he does for a lot of people.

"They call this ship a rust bucket, but I don't think it's a rust bucket. I like this ship a lot. This is the best one I been on. I like to work, and if I know the overtime's thrown at me I'll work even more. If I work a lotta lotta overtime I'll get like $5,000 a month. Tax taken out I get $3,300 to $3,400. $3,400 times twelve, it's quite a sum, you know that? I don't have the strength to work like that every day. Sometimes I get tired and fall asleep.

"I like the old-style winches, a lot of electrical gear, and man, so much electricity on here and so much to learn it's unbelievable. The other ships are mostly automated and ain't really nothing there to learn. Here it's better. There were crews I been with that weren't too hot. But this is much more better than bein' where a lot of people are. Like they all join together and go against you. I like it out here. As long as they don't get in my way I don't bother them, they don't bother me. That's the way I am. If you bother me, I'm gonna fight back. I'm a simple man."

Floggings
to Loggings

MR. DARBY TOOK HIS PROBLEM TO THE CAPTAIN, WHO WAS SYM-
pathetic. He said he would keep the pistol for him in the ship's
safe, along with his own. He told the Chief Mate to enter it into
the ship's stores declaration. He eased Mr. Darby's fear by telling
him that this seemed a "happy crew," more or less, and that he'd
seen much, much worse. You could tell that from going through
the ship's files.

DATE OF OFFENSE: JULY 4, 1976
LOCATION: DAMMAN, SAUDI ARABIA
TIME: 2325

OFFENSE COMMITTED: At about 2325 July 4, 1976 AB Gregory Bender
after previously threatening to beat OS Hernando Borja OS did together
with EU [Engine Utilityman] Michael Vock inflict severe head and
chest injurys by beating kicking and stomping Borja until he was unconscious in the crews messroom.

CHARGES PREFERRED BY: CAPTAIN DIGBY LEE
WITNESS TO OFFENSE: CH. MATE H. PITT HARDING

ACTION TAKEN: Fined one days pay amounting to $24.13
Refer this brutal assault to US consul, USCG, and
SIU union for further action
We did proceed to Berth #5 Damman all secure at 1600 July 10, 1976.
The next day at 1000 Mr. Engelken U.S. Consul Rep did come aboard
and finish the interrogation. Bender and Vock were signed Off Due

83

Misconduct. Vock is by his own admission on Parole for some prior offense. We can do without this, and should make an all out effort to rid our vessels of these two people in the future.

At the time of this incident, the *Columbianna* had been at anchor off Damman for twenty-five days awaiting cargo. The temperature inside was ninety-five during the day, ninety at night. On deck, it could hit one hundred and ten. If the crew went ashore in the launch, the single diversion was an out-of-order Coca-Cola machine at the end of the pier. Even that was closely watched by Saudi harbor police toting machine guns.

Vock and Bender put a hole in Borja's left cheek, which according to the Captain, was "so big you could put two fingers through it." It took thirty-seven stitches to close all his wounds. Vock and Bender were read the charges by the Captain in the presence of the Bosun, who is the unlicensed crew's union representative on board. Vock could neither read nor write but said he understood the charges. The Captain was especially glad to be rid of Bender, a former Green Beret who served in Vietnam. One month earlier he had attacked another crew member in Assab, Ethiopia. "Sailing coastwise is one thing," the Captain said, "but you get these guys over to the Persian Gulf an' they get all squirrelly."

In cases of misconduct, the company does not have to pay airfare back to the States. "I made that son of a bitch pay his own way back," the Captain recalled with obvious satisfaction. "Thirteen *hunnerd* dollars."

The proximate cause of all this had been the volume of Borja's radio.

Vock is still sailing. Not long after the incident, Bender, driving along a country road at night, slammed into a tree. He pulled himself free of the wreck, but, unable to walk, he lay down beside it and died of loss of blood during the night.

Another file told of a troublesome cook who served on the *Columbianna.*

Mr. Binks joined the *Columbianna* June 1, 1978 Bayonne N.J. for this voyage. Ch. Steward related to me that he had Binks as Ch. Cook on another vessel some time ago and had to send him home due to violent temper and actions when drinking.

I had several complaints during the voyage from G. Austin 3rd cook about Binks and also R. Cavalcanti 2nd Ck. Upon arriving Suez, Cavalcanti complained about Varicose Veins in his leg bleeding and succeeded in getting off NFFD [Not Fit For Duty].

Prior arriving at Subic Bay I requested a 2nd Cook and Baker from Agent C.F. Sharp. They supplied a Philippino man Segundo Chavez U.S. Citizen with proper Seamans Document Passport etc. He went to work 7/18 and quit 7/19. Mr. Chavez stated that he valued his Life more than the job.

The voyage proceeded via Pusan, Guam then Midway with a few minor complaints enroute. At Midway however Binks did not turn to after arrival Aug 10/78, and stayed continuously under the influence of Alcoholic Beverages. I searched his room on three different occasions during his last 5 days on ship, a no-work no-pay period for Binks. I confiscated 2 bottles Gin & 2 cases beer one time and 1 Scotch another time and upon his Departure found 5 empty fifths of various whiskies in his quarters. Binks's quarters were adjacent to Dock and people were supplying him through porthole. Almost impossible to stop.

Binks upon occasion would appear around or near the mess and threaten the Steward and others there, then leave. I witnessed this on two different occasions during this 5 day period I decided to send Binks home on the 14th of Aug. I gave Binks an additional $100.00 draw and he left with his gear without incident about 0830 Aug 15 saying that he hoped he hadn't caused me any problem.

I believe that Binks needs another company to work for besides this one and suggest he not be rehired in the future.

The Captain hated paperwork, but collected these written statements for a practical reason: he was afraid of being sued. Captains these days are frequently hauled into court by seamen they fire and charged with unjust termination of employment. A lot of captains—the *Columbianna*'s included—are terribly reluctant to discipline a man, since it so often leads to lawsuits and

85

lawyers. If this seems odd, it may help to consider the way it used to be.

The *San Francisco Chronicle* ran a story on March 14, 1882, about the treatment of the crew by the mates of the American ship *Gatherer:*

> On the 15th of the month on which the vessel sailed, Curtis the second mate, so dealt with John Hansen that one of his eyes was nearly put out, and his mouth so badly injured that he can scarcely eat or speak. On the 20th of the same month John Burns was lashed to the rail and Watts [the first mate] broke his nose and disfigured him with brass knuckles. A boy standing by interfered and was struck by the mate on the head. . . . The mate also struck the steward of the ship over the head and put him in confinement and kept him without food for five days. He was landed at San Pedro a lunatic, and is now confined at Los Angeles. On November 15th McCue being partially stripped was fastened by a strap to his waist and raised up to the mizzen stay and held head downward until he was black in the face from the rush of blood to his head.

A contemporary British book on the life of men aboard the "Yankee hellships" noted that aside from "ribs stamped in by heavy seaboots" and "faces smashed like rotten apples by iron belaying pins . . . there have been many instances of men triced up [suspended off the deck] in the rigging, stripped, and then literally skinned alive with deck scrapers."

Suicide was not uncommon on these ships. The above may be especially brutal examples, but they are not unrepresentative. And by the late nineteenth century things were a lot better than they had been.

Flogging was outlawed by federal statute in 1850, but that only encouraged other, more enterprising, forms of discipline that made flogging seem benign. In 1898 corporal punishment in all forms was finally outlawed aboard U.S. ships. Only one year before that, the Supreme Court had declared that the Thirteenth Amendment, which makes involuntary servitude illegal, did not apply to seamen. Not until 1915 was the American merchant

86

seaman really emancipated. On March 4 of that year President Wilson signed into law the Seaman's Act, which was pushed through Congress by Sen. Robert "Fighting Bob" La Follette of Wisconsin. This bill, which came to be called "the Magna Carta of the Sea," limited the seaman's work week to fifty-six hours; guaranteed certain minimum living standards, such as a quart of water per man per day; and abolished imprisonment for desertion. Another provision required that at least seventy-five percent of the crewmen had to be able to "understand orders": conditions had become so deplorable that the crews of U.S. ships were largely made up of foreigners—rough, tough Germans, Swedes, Norwegians, Dutchmen, and Russian Finns. Very often one couldn't understand the other. This had an unfortunate effect in many emergencies.

These days discipline is divided into two categories: "dry" and "wet." This has nothing to do with keelhauling. There are two kinds of logbook. The "dry" log is where the captain might record minor infractions, such as drunkenness, or not turning to. If a man is docked a day's pay or more, it is noted in the dry log. But the "wet" log—the official logbook of the United States Coast Guard—is for recording serious breaches of discipline. This one is sent to Coast Guard headquarters in Washington.

The Captain only wet-logs a man if his patience is sorely tried, though once he got so mad at a crew he wet-logged practically the lot of them. They had been causing trouble all voyage long, and toward its end, when fifteen of them didn't show up at sailing time, the Captain wrote all their names down in the log.

"Somethin' of a record, I believe," he said.

Their union patrolman, the ombudsman who argues on their behalf in such cases, came down to the ship from the union hall and informed the Captain he would "allow" him five loggings, but not fifteen, no way.

"To hell with that," the Captain told the patrolman.

"May be," he replied, "but you log fifteen of 'em and next time you need a crew, you won't get one. I'll see to that *personally.*"

On hearing this the company paymaster said, "Oh, for God-sakes, no, not that," and had a fit.

The patrolman, having made his point, went below and selected five men whom he "allowed" the Captain to log.

In the case of Mr. Binks, the Captain took additional statements—against the possibility Mr. Binks might have been waiting on the dock with a lawyer when the *Columbianna* arrived back in the United States. The final statement is that of the Chief Steward, Slim's father.

STATEMENT FROM BENJAMIN GREEN, CHIEF STEWARD
REGARDS MARVIN BINKS

In regards to Mr. Binks, there had been a number of time when he had come in the galley when he was drinking that he had told me that he we was not going to do like Souza did. He said that I have better get ready, because he was not taking anymore mess off of me and the B/R. I think that Mr. Binks should be put in the School in Piney Points for his drinking problem. Mr. Binks said time and time again that he was going to do to me what Souza did to me. See, Souza is the one that damn about cook me alive on the last ship I was on. I think something should be did in order to stop Mr. Binks.

One *Minute's* Silence
_____*for Paul Hall*

ONCE A WEEK, AFTER SUPPER, THERE WAS A UNION MEETING IN
the messhall for the unlicensed crew members. The officers have
their own unions. The Chief Steward presided, and opened by
asking if there were any beefs to discuss. A beef is the union term
for a complaint. Before anyone had a chance to speak, the Ghost
got up.

"Nooooo," he said, in his heavy Norwegian accent, "no beefs
I can tink ov. I been tinking dat ve all vurk for a living, and have
jobs to do. An I tink ve should all be tankful ve *have* jobs. An dat
ve get *paid* for dem—"

"*Amen*, brother," said the Steward, cutting him off. "Is
there any other business?"

The Bosun said yes, he had a beef. J. D. and Kirk, two
Ordinaries, were complaining to the Captain that the Bosun was
taking all the overtime for himself.

"Bulllllll*shit,*" said J. D.

"Ain' no bullshit," said the Bosun.

"Bulllllll*shit.*"

"Ain' no bullshit."

This continued until the Steward held up his hand and in
his fog-cutter voice said, "Okay, what we got here is a beef, but
I'm supposed to take the beefs to the Captain, not just anyone.
Th' Old Man has enough stuff comin' down on his ass." That was
true.

There were no more beefs, so they stood and, as is the Seafarers International Union tradition at the end of shipboard union meetings, a held a moment of silence for all dead seafaring brothers.

By 9:00 A.M. on June 25, 1980, it was already hot in Brooklyn. Secret Service agents had opened their station wagon and were unloading green plastic cases that held the Uzis and whatever else they need to protect vice-presidents. Police were trying to monitor traffic by the Seafarers International Union hall, now jammed with mourners. The flower cars were causing the bottleneck. Seven of them were double-parked out front. Limousines were lining up behind them. The Secret Service was trying to get the flower cars moved back.

Anthony Scotto, president of the Brooklyn International Longshoremen's Association Local 1814, had just arrived. He had recently been convicted of bribery, extortion, and racketeering. The Honorable John M. Murphy, Democratic congressman from Staten Island, chairman of the House Merchant Marine and Fisheries Committee, arrived shortly after Mr. Scotto, looking solemn, but with a smile for a few old friends. He was busy campaigning for a tenth term in Congress and trying to get his ABSCAM trial ended quickly. He was understandably anxious, inasmuch as it is inconvenient to campaign for public office while the nation is watching videotapes of you accepting a bribe from an undercover FBI agent posing as a sheik.

"They are burying an ethic at Paul Hall's funeral in the Seafarers International Union headquarters today," Murray Kempton had written that morning of June 25 in his *New York Post* column. "Paul Hall was the labor leader who stood by Mr. Nixon until the ship went down."

Paul Hall was an extraordinary man, and had the cancer not set in over a year earlier, he probably would have succeeded George Meany as president of the AFL-CIO. As it was, Meany held on too long, Hall not long enough. When Meany finally picked Lane Kirkland, a former third mate in the merchant marine, it was with the hope that Hall would live long enough to

90

watch over Kirkland until he had earned the respect of the AFL-CIO Executive Council.

Paul Hall was born in 1915 near Birmingham, Alabama, and caught his first ship in the thirties. He began as a wiper, earning $1.60 a day. A wiper—the low man in the engine room—today earns about $30.00 a day on a U.S. ship. Hall's work helped make the difference.

The thirties were a stormy, bloody time in American maritime labor history. The trouble began in 1934 with a series of scattered "job actions" that two years later developed into the strike of 1936–1937. It was a bitter nine-week period of lockouts, killings, and police confrontations that lasted through an unusually cold winter. Finally, on January 24, forty-one shipping companies agreed to a ten-dollar-a-month raise, a basic seventy-cent hourly overtime rate, and the union hiring hall system, whereby the unions would supply ships with crews drawn from their membership. It was a decisive victory for the seamen. But during the strike the NMU had accepted a lot of support from the Communist Workers party. When the Party wanted to continue the strike, even though most of the seamen's demands had been met, the Communists' ambitions for the NMU and the American labor movement became clear. And so, in November 1938, William Green, then president of the American Federation of Labor, persuaded Harry Lundeberg, a Norwegian-born seaman and union leader, to found a union to counter the Communist-dominated National Maritime. Paul Hall, deeply anti-Communist after the experience of that long, cold winter, joined the group of five hundred men who organized the SIU.

Thinking back on the old days, Hall told a reporter in 1966, "There are a lot of reasons not to like the Commies, but one of the best is they are a bunch of finks. They didn't give a damn about the labor movement. We showed the men that. One thing about sailors, they may not be well-educated, but they aren't stupid."

During the war, Hall shipped as an oiler and later became a New York port agent for the SIU, as well as the director of

Organization. He was involved in setting up the Maritime Trades Department within the AFL-CIO, an alliance of unions that has grown to 8 million members, most of them ironworkers, plumbers, and painters who have no connection with the sea. In time, the Maritime Trades Department became Hall's personal fiefdom. By then the problem was not Communists but the mob. Hall fought them too and by 1949 he was an important enough adversary to be framed with heroin planted in his car. By 1954 he was important enough to kill: on December 23 that year James Cobb was arrested outside Hall's home with a loaded shotgun. He pleaded guilty to conspiracy to murder. In 1957, Harry Lundeberg died, and Hall became president of the SIU and Maritime Trades.

He was a fighting man, wrote Kempton, who "let everybody know that when he took up the sword, he threw away the scabbard," displaying a "posture in confrontation that would have done credit to the Archangel Michael." Meany would often call on him to help persuade management of the virtues of a new pension plan or some other scheme. Hall would enter the office and sit quietly in an armchair in the rear, listening to the management types complain. Then Meany would lift his cigar, as a signal, and Hall would say, "Now, sir, you seem to be an intelligent man. I don't understand why you're acting like such a *dopey cocksucker.*" He got a lot done that way.

There is a story about how he broke in a new man. Once a young SIU employee, just promoted from port agent to Washington lobbyist, got a phone call from Hall at 1:30 A.M.

"How're you doing, son?" said Hall.

"Uh, fine, sir," he replied, terrified.

Next night Hall called at 2:30 A.M. "just to ask your feeling about a bill." The young man described his feelings as best he could.

Two nights later Hall called at 3:15 A.M. "to have a casual talk."

"Jesus Christ, Paul," the man said, "can't this wait until morning?"

"Glad to hear that, son," said Hall. "Just testing your common sense, wanted to see how much crap you'd take."

In 1967 he engineered a real feat by setting up the Harry Lundeberg School of Seamanship at Piney Point, Maryland, a center that trains unskilled and often illiterate young men and women for seafaring careers. The Lundeberg School is tightly run, has an alcohol rehabilitation program, and teaches remedial reading and writing. Piney Point is entirely paid for by American shipping companies that employ SIU seamen. The shipping companies may not be getting much out of Piney Point, since almost all of its graduates leave the merchant marine within a year, but the shipping companies are not asked for their opinion. Hall's other accomplishments—looking at it from the union's point of view—include the fifty-fifty preference law by which the U.S. government must ship at least half its cargoes on U.S. flag vessels; preserving the Jones Act, which requires that cargoes shipped between two consecutive U.S. ports be carried only on American ships; the Merchant Marine Act of 1970, providing federal subsidies for the building of three hundred new ships over ten years; and the continued operation of U.S. Public Health Service facilities for seamen. The SIU also claims the Alaska pipeline as one of his triumphs, although that is stretching it some. At the time of Hall's death, the SIU could boast a membership of ninety thousand.

By 11:00 A.M. everyone had arrived and paid respects to Mr. Hall's widow, Rose, their son and daughter. Scotto and Murphy had chatted together briefly in the aisle. Rival union leaders had said hello to each other. Frank Drozak, Hall's taciturn successor, shook hands and kept a firm jaw. The Secret Service men watched from the balcony and aisles. Some old sailors, who weren't allowed to sit in chairs saved for VIPs, cried. They were the real mourners. When a ship's bell struck the hour, Vice-President Mondale moved to the podium to give the first eulogy.

It was an election year; if Carter hadn't been in Yugoslavia, he probably would have attended himself. Mondale said that Hall had loved his country and that his country had loved him back, that there hadn't been a decent cause he hadn't worked for, and that if Paul had talked bluntly it was "because he wanted you to know how he thought." Mondale added, "If he stuck by his

93

friend, and he did, it was because loyalty, to him, was deeper than fashion." He said he'd just spoken with the president, who'd asked him to convey the message that he had lost one of his "closest advisors" and that "Paul was a man of integrity." He closed by saying Paul had loved to read anything that had to do with the sea, and "recalled something Paul knew by heart" and read the first stanza of Masefield's "Sea Fever."

Hugh Carey, the governor of New York, then gave his eulogy. He said that Hall "believed the Bill of Rights meant what it said," and that ". . . death is too weak a thing to obliterate the greatness of this man." Carey remembered "the hours he spent with me here in this hall, sharing his dreams about labor," and concluded by sharing with all his concept of Heaven. "My idea of Heaven," he said, "is a place that combines the sea, Brooklyn, and Piney Point . . . the seraphim and the cherabim and the seamen will be standing there beside George Meany and Harry Lundeberg, and Paul will be standing right behind them."

Lane Kirkland was the last to talk, briefly, and without political reference, except for the reminder that "this nation can't hope to survive the disappearance of the brotherhood of the sea . . . the chance for American men to go down to the sea in ships." He spoke with real affection, it seemed, as he closed, saying, "That big red Alabaman heart of Paul Hall's is now still, but the strong beat of it carries on. Take it on the slow bell, Paul. We'll not see your like again."

At graveside, by a pond in Greenwood Cemetery, last words were said over the coffin.

Hall's death left a power vacuum in maritime labor at a time when jobs and ships and image were at an historical low. He is survived by a lot of hungry men, who may not have his kind of guts or his kind of ethic. "I did not say that Paul Hall's ethic could not on occasion be outrageous," wrote Murray Kempton, referring to Hall's standing by Nixon to the end, but "it is a poor ethic that can't drive its possessor to look outrageous now and then. And Paul Hall's ethic was the grandest I have ever known."

Toward the end, a voice may have whispered to him that death is greater than life and does obliterate greatness, making dust of deckhands, governors, and presidents alike. Whatever voice it was, it spoke to him through the coma brought on by the brain tumor that was to kill him. Shortly before he died, Paul Hall awoke, conscious even in his last moments that life is cruel, and said to his wife, "Don't let those fuckers screw you out of my pension."

May such a man rest in peace.

Tightened Ship

BY THE TIME THE LAST OF THE GALES ABATED, ANOTHER U.S. embassy (this one in Libya) had been sacked, terrorists had killed two American navy seamen and wounded ten more in an ambush at Sabana Seca, Puerto Rico, and cargo had shifted in the number three hold. It was all bad news. Mr. Dexter decided it was just a matter of time before the _Columbianna_ was dispatched to the Gulf. Higgin shook his head over the murdered navy men. Rocco declared the incidents further portents of apocalypse, and increased to two hundred his daily regimen of push-ups.

All the lashings in the number three hold had worked loose, allowing one of the M-60 tanks to slide a foot. These tanks weighed forty-seven tons apiece. Loose cargo is one of the worst dangers on a ship. During the Vietnam sealift, a ship called the _Badger State_ ran into a bad storm while carrying a load of B-52 bombs. One of them, stored athwartship, broke free and slammed through the _Badger_'s side. It didn't detonate, but it did put a hole in her hull. She began to take on water. The order to abandon was given; the crew made it into the lifeboat. But as the lifeboat passed under the hole made by the bomb, another bomb slid through it, fell into the lifeboat, and sank it. Three men survived. Mr. Fogarty, the seventy-year-old Chief Mate with the grin that made people nervous, had been on a ship that picked up the _Badger_'s distress signals. He tended to worry about shifting cargo more than he did about the absence of thermometers.

97

Now the lashings had to be tightened. No one was anxious to go down into the number three. There were about forty tanks in rows two feet apart. The men would have to inch along the spaces between the treads with screwdrivers and flashlights to get at the turnbuckles on the cables. In the still-rolling ship, it was tricky work. The toothlike edges on the tank treads made it worse. There were no overhead lights in the number three—Rocco had not gotten around to fixing them yet—and its dark, cavernous insides echoed with the straining of steel.

The work paid $8.17 extra per hour. The union considers securing cargo a penalty-rate job. The SIU contract specifies extra pay for dirty or dangerous work, such as topping or lowering booms, tossing garbage, tending livestock, removing soot from the stack, or working with carbon tetrachloride, TNT, nitroglycerine, cyanide, copra, lampblack, manure, bones, green hides. Even lifeboat drill held on a Saturday, Sunday, or holiday is subject to the penalty rate.

Higgin, Bob Cascabel, Pooch, the Bosun, and the rest of the deck crew went down together into the number three. Only Charley Eastman refused. He was an Ordinary Seaman on the four-to-eight watch. Charley was fifty-one, looked about seventy. He was missing seven front teeth. It was hard to understand what Charley said. His voice was a phlegmy burble from a lifetime of booze and smokes. Some nights he kept Higgin, who had the bunk above him, awake with his coughing fits. The night before, Higgin had timed one of them at four minutes. When it was over, Charley lit a cigarette.

"Je-sus Chr-*ayst*, Charley," said Higgin, "why doncha light *another* one?"

Charley told Higgin he had emphysema anyway and when he died the union was going to give his wife Louella thirty *thousand* dollars. "Well," said Higgin later, "there's no way the union is gonna give his wife that kind of money.

"But ol' Charley changed his tune. The order came to go down into the hold and tighten the tanks, and he said, 'I ain't goin'. Go ahead an' log me, I ain't goin'. I ain't goin' down there until they call out the Steward's department an' the Cook's department, the Mates an' the Master. Until there's danger o' sinkin'.' "

The men emerged from the hold several hours later, squinting into the late afternoon sun. Pooch was holding his stomach and looking distressed, either from the motion or the old knife wound. More likely the latter. They were exhausted and ready to knock off even if it was a bit early. Before crawling in between the tanks, they had listened for five minutes to the noises, memorizing the rhythm. Then, if they heard a sound that didn't belong, they could jump away fast. Their muscles were stiff from tensing. Higgin's calves ached. Lee Roland had hit his elbow on a machine-gun turret as he leaped out of the way of what he thought was converging heavy machinery. They were all ready for long hot showers.

Mr. Dexter padded about the corridors in bare feet and oversized boxer shorts. He never used a laundry bag. He undressed right in front of the washing machine, threw in his clothes, and walked back to his cabin in his undershorts. He'd change into new undershorts, walk back to the washing machine, and throw in the dirty ones. It was a daily ritual.

The watch had changed. It was the quiet hour before supper, Sparks was in his cabin, wastebasket full of ice and beer at his feet, leaning back in his armchair reading *Blood Horse* magazine, smoking his forty-fifth Pall Mall of the day. The Captain was in the head (his bathroom), trying to maneuver a Q-tip soaked in anesthetic back onto an abcessed gum. It was difficult because of the size of his fingers. The Chief Steward was taking the fourth of five daily showers, letting the water run soothingly over the scar tissue from the burn that covered half his chest and back. Yoya, having convinced one of the engineers that if he didn't get something to drink he would put dishwater in the engineers' coffee urn, was now taking a long bracing pull on a bottle of Old Mr. Boston rye whiskey. Yannos, the baker who spoke to no one, chewed on a toothpick and waited for his bread to rise. The Bosun hand-rolled a supply of cigarettes for the evening's poker game. The Second walked the bridge, sextant in hand, preparing to shoot the stars. Mr. Darby was writing to his mother, telling her how much he hated the Second. Chiefy was lying on his bed, forearm over his eyes, trying to remember where he had stored the extra muff joints. Jefferson was smoking grass with Rick, the wall-eyed messman. Rocco was checking the relay switches in the forward winch house. Slim and Gut were setting tables.

Higgin had finished his shower and poured the last inch of his Myers's rum into a glass. J.D. was gobbing on a whetstone, putting the edge back on his knife. Charley Eastman was lying on his bunk, smoking. Bob Cascabel was adding up the scribbles on his overtime sheet: a bit over a thousand dollars in one week of fifteen-hour days. An Ordinary called Dogbreath was on the poop deck with a tape recorder, playing Teena Marie to the North Atlantic as he hit the punching bag. Big Mac, the old chief gunner's mate, was in his focsle applying Vaseline to his cancerous lower lip. The Yanson brothers were taping the hospital walls with color tear sheets from *Hustler* and *Penthouse,* and talking about reducing the noise level on Gary's homemade helicopter by using a larger butane canister as a muffler. Marty was opening five-gallon tins of sauerkraut. Pooch was running out of Tagamet. Ranly, one of the engineers, was trying to get the news on the shortwave band. He preferred Armed Forces Radio and Voice of America to Radio Moscow, but this close to Europe, Radio Moscow's signal was stronger.

The announcer's mellifluous voice, with an English accent, spilled into the passageway through Ranly's open door. She began this evening with a report on the attack against the U.S. Navy base in Puerto Rico by "revolutionaries in the struggle against imperialism." Ranly scratched himself and yawned. "She left out the U.S.," he said. "Usually she says 'U.S. imperialism.' " He thought about it for a moment and said "I suppose it's implicit." He twiddled with the dials and after a lot of *weeeeeeooooooooo-weeeooooooooo* ing of shortwaves ricocheting off the ionosphere, brought in a crackly Armed Forces Radio broadcast. The announcer said the Saudis had reopened the Grand Mosque in Mecca.

Higgin was looking over the menu when Eckert walked in wearing an undershirt—the scoop-necked, sleeveless kind.

"Hey, c'mon, goddammit," Higgin said.

"Huh?" said Eckert.

"How 'bout puttin' on a shirt?"

"I'm wearing a shirt."

"I mean a real shirt."

"This is a real shirt."

"C'mon, man," said Higgin, "I get enough hair in my food around here without havin' to stare at your armpits while I eat." Higgin knew how to appeal to a man's sympathy.

"All right," said Eckert, shuffling off.

"I'm gonna have to have a *long* talk with that boy," said Higgin to Cascabel. He continued reading his menu. The choices were roast prime ribs, kielbasa with steamed sauerkraut, or creole-style smoked pork hocks in sauce. He told Gut to bring him the beef, baked potato, asparagus, and garlic bread.

"Okay, babe," said Gut, who called all the white crewmen either *babe* or *Craig*. Gut said most white people were named Craig, so he found it safe to call them that.

"An' hold the hair."

Higgin wasn't squeamish. Far from it. In eleven years with the navy, he had seen a lot of peculiar things done with food. The baker on one of his nuclear subs had been caught in flagrante delicto with a French roll hot out of the oven. But he said he had never seen so many hairs in his food as he had on this ship. It did nothing for crew morale. This morning his eggs arrived sunny-side-up, one of them with a little gray curly hair exactly in mid-yolk. The other yolk had a black, kinky hair just off center.

"You know what they say about that?" said Big Mac from across the table. He had twenty-eight years in the navy. New York Irish, son of a cop.

"What's that?" said Higgin.

"The good Lord sends the food, and the devil sends the cook."

J. D. asked when the English channel pilot would come

aboard. Ships traveling through the English channel are now required to take on pilots. Cascabel said tomorrow, around 1500.

In the officers' mess, there was a lack of conversation at the Captain's table. This table was for the Captain and his two chief officers. But the three men sitting at it had no pleasantries to relate; and if they spoke at all, it was about ship's business. Chief Engineer Muzzio's eyes seldom left his plate. Chiefy looked depleted, tired, a bit forlorn. He had cut off the tip of his thumb on a gear tooth. After three days of engine room wear and tear the gauze bandage looked like the funeral wrapping on King Tut. Every fourth or fifth slurp, an unraveled bit dipped into his pea soup.

"Chief," said the Captain finally, "I'd like you to stow those barrels of oil you got on deck. They start rollin' around, someone's liable to get hurt."

"I can't do it today," said Chiefy. "I'm beat. I was up till two-thirty in the morning workin' on the condenser."

The Captain looked at him. "I'm not askin' you to do it *personally*, Chief. You got thirteen people working for you. One of them can do it."

"Well," said Chiefy, "I don't know what kind of oil it is." This being not exactly relevant to moving the barrels, the Captain's face went the color of a Harvard beet.

"It's goddamned HD-30! It's what you wrote on the outside of it."

Halfway through his chocolate chip ice cream, the chief mate, Mr. Fogarty, who had not yet spoken, said to the Captain, "I hear we're going to Karachi."

The Captain looked at him blankly. "Oh? Well, I ain't heard nothin' about Karachi."

"I've heard some very persistent rumors," said the Chief Mate.

"Like what?" said the Captain, careful not to take his eyes off his food.

"Well, that we're going to pick up a load of ammunition in Bremerhaven and then go to Karachi."

The Captain considered this as he pulled a chunk of pineapple from his Jell-O. "Don't start any nasty rumors, Mate."

"Nasty rumors?" said the Chief. "Nothing nasty about them. You're just the last to hear them."

_Schadenfreude_*

"YOU NEVER _SEEN_ A MAN LOOK SO GLUM," SAID THE CHIEF MATE
afterward of the effect his Karachi rumor had on the Captain. Of
course he had made up the rumor from scratch—he'd use any
excuse to perturb the Captain. It was easy on a tramp, since no
one knew for sure where she was going next. Whenever he was
particularly annoyed with the Captain, the Chief would insinuate
the dread specter of the Persian Gulf. Karachi was close enough
for discomfort.

The Chief was a master at getting captains off his back. He
once talked about "another terrible" captain he'd served under on
a freighter during the Vietnam war. This particular captain, he
said, was "easily frightened" by explosions. He found that by
dropping concussion grenades into the water, he could terrify him
into retreating to his cabin for hours. Unfortunately he ran out
of grenades. It was probably for the best that the weapons on the
Columbianna were locked inside sealed containers.

The Captain and the Chief loved to regale people with
stories of each other's incompetence, cowardice, immorality, de-
bility, whatever. Here Mr. Fogarty had the advantage of Captain
Lee, because on a ship, ultimately everything is the Captain's
responsibility. When $120,000 worth of anchor chain zipped
through the hawsepipe and fell irretrievably to the bottom of the

_____
*A mischievous delight in the misfortune of another.

Gulf of Aqaba because of a rusted-away winch brake, the Chief's mood brightened for days. Even now, three years later, the memory was still bright. But his happiest recollection was the time in Bandar-e Shahpur, especially the moments when he had the Captain convinced he was going to be killed. Such glee in someone else's misery was strange in a man so outwardly benign. It didn't go with the gray wisps of hair, the specs, the smile, the voice never raised above a whisper. Mr. Fogarty began the story of Iran:

"Here we are in the harbor, the only American ship in port. The Captain didn't have any idea what we were doing. A major, a captain, and a sergeant in the Shah's army come by. They looked like field marshals, wearing all these medals and braid. Swagger sticks. The major explained the situation was getting kind of desperate. Everyone in the country had been on strike for three months. He said, 'I don't think we can get any longshoremen, but we'll try to come up with something.' We had to unload these CBUs [Cluster Bomb Units]. Mr. Mobasser came down. He'd been working for Iran-Amer for eighteen years. That was the agency handled all the American ships. He talked it over with the major and the captain, trying to figure out how to get some people to do the discharging. They all had drinks up in the Captain's cabin, getting relaxed.

"The fourth day the government collapsed, and here we are with these CBUs. By this time we'd started some discharging. They had college kids, high school kids off the street, and old men, anyone they could find. Taking CBUs out of the number four, piling them on the dock. Hauling them off in old camel carts. It was kind of a primitive operation.

"So then five days later—it was Saint Valentine's Day—they sacked the embassy. The Iranian captain came down to tell us about it. We'd already heard it on Radio Kuwait. Our Captain didn't want to hear *any* of this stuff. All he wanted to do was get out of there. He was so nervous he couldn't talk. He couldn't eat. He had a hard time even *drinking*. And he kept calling me on the intercom. He never called me up to his room. Hard-assing me, like he always does. When he started that I said, 'Did you hear Radio

Kuwait?' I thought he was going to explode any minute. I said, 'Radio Kuwait says the embassy fell and they killed all these people.'

"When the Iranian captain came down he was wearing blue jeans. Said he was trying to keep a low profile. I says, 'Where's the major?' He said the major was hanged, or was going to be. 'They got the majors. Captains are next.' I says, 'What about Mr. Mobasser?' He said he was in the hospital, he was a casualty of the shooting.

"A day or so later he comes down to the ship again. Discharging was going slowly. I says, 'How's Mr. Mobasser?' 'Oh,' he said, 'that was very bad.' He said the mob came up to his hospital bed and they stuck a .45 in his head and made him confess that he was a collaborator with the U.S. because he'd been working with this agency for eighteen years. It was either confess or have his head blown off, one or the other. So he said he was. And they took him out of his bunk, dragged him through the streets, and got him to the square, hitting him more and more, and stuck him on a spike on an iron fence, and before he died, while he's screaming and hollering, they put a big sign on him in Iranian saying 'U.S. Collaborator.' I says, 'That wasn't a very nice thing to do, was it?' He said, 'The mobs are going crazy.'

"Everything was chaotic—everything. About noon a few days later the Captain calls the Chief Engineer [Chiefy] and myself up to his office. He says, 'We're gonna pull out of here tonight. I'm gonna leave here tonight. When it gets dark. He asks Muzzio, 'Whaddya think of that?' Muzzio says, 'Yeah, let's get the hell out of here.' He didn't ask me. But they both knew what I was gonna say. I said, 'You know what's gonna happen? First of all, you gotta get down that river. *If* you can get away from the dock, you've still gotta get down that river. You've got all these cannonballs in the number four, they can go up in smoke. What if you hit that shoal down river? You're gonna have one big funeral right here.' And I said, 'What're you gonna do for a pilot?'

"The Captain said, 'We'll use the same one brought us in.'

"I said, 'You know where that pilot is?'

"He said, 'Where?'

"I said, 'They hanged him two days ago.'

" 'Oh my God,' he says. 'What're we gonna *do?*'

"I said, 'That gunboat that took us in, you know where it is? It's down by that shoal waiting for you. He's gonna turn you back and bring you right back to this dock. If you're lucky he'll put soldiers on board and put you under house arrest. But if you're not so lucky he's gonna hang your ass to that radar mast right up there.' "

The Chief Mate chuckled. "I thought he was gonna have a heart attack. So he says, 'Go away! Leave me alone! Go away! Go away!'

"The next evening he called me and Muzzio up to his cabin. He wanted Muzzio there because he would echo what he wanted to say. And he said, 'Well, I've decided I'm leaving now, as soon as it gets dark. You secure this cargo somehow.' I said, 'Captain, your life isn't worth a plug nickel if you leave this dock. You know that. I know that. We all know that.'

"I told him all these gory things that were going to happen to him. After he sat down sobbing, I thought I'd reassure him. I said, 'Captain, look at it this way, we all have to die. What better way of dying than to have your throat slit with a *really* sharp knife?'

" 'Oh my God!' he said. 'Get out of here!'

"He wasn't reassured at all. He would've rather I hadn't even said anything at all," said Mr. Fogarty, almost surprised.

"I could get on him. I knew that I was protected, see. I knew that all that was around me was protected. I felt that very strongly."

With the last of the cluster bombs unloaded, the Iranian army captain told the Captain on February 18 to leave Bandar-e Shahpur right away and arranged a gunboat escort down river. It was that same day the Captain received the Flash precedence cable from his charterers at the Pentagon directing him to "cease cargo ops" and "depart Bandar Shahpur ASAP." The last message he had had from Washington was a cable the day after he arrived in Bandar-e Shahpur on February 5, advising him "do not enter Bandar Shahpur." As the *Columbianna* steamed out the Strait of Hormuz bound for Suez, another cable arrived, well deserved.

CONGRATULATIONS ARE DUE YOU AND YOUR COLUM-BIANNA CREW FOR AGAIN DEMONSTRATING THAT LEGEND-ARY AMERICAN INGENUITY STILL EXIST YOUR DISCHARGING OF DANGEROUS CARGO IN AN AREA IN TURMOIL IN A PORT WHERE THERE WAS NO UNITED STATES REPRESENTATION AND AT A TIME WHEN COMMUNICATION WITH LOCAL AU-THORITIES AND U.S. GOVERNMENT OFFICIALS WAS EX-TREMELY DIFFICULT AGAIN DEMONSTRATES THAT REAL PROS GET THE JOB DONE NO MATTER WHAT THE CHAL-LENGE THE TOUGHER THE TASK THE HARDER THEY WORK AND THE BETTER THEIR PERFORMANCE PLEASE PASS MY CONGRATULATIONS TO EVERY MAN IN YOUR CREW FOR A JOB WELL DONE—RADM [Rear Admiral] TIERNEY, U.S. NAVY

Mr. Fogarty's sense of humor was as dry as faggots piled around a stake. Talking about death seemed to raise his spirits. He felt a clinical fascination in the sound people made when their throats were cut, the smell of a body turned up with the tide. One night after a supper of Yoya's braised lamb, he mentioned casually how much the taste reminded him of human flesh.

He had held forty-four different jobs in his lifetime. He had run a trading post for Navaho Indians, a rabbit ranch, a rattle-snake farm, the Guam public school system. He'd written four books on mathematics, one on typing. He'd taught O. J. Simpson how to type at a business school in San Diego. He'd taught business administration at San Diego State. He'd been a cop. In 1937, he came up with the idea for the first shock-therapy training program for bad drivers in the United States. He'd dug ditches; embalmed corpses—including his infant son's; sold cars, maga-zine subscriptions, real estate. He'd been a mercenary. He had married and raised a family but had never stopped wandering, and had always ended up out of money and back at sea.

He was born in Arizona in 1914, two years after it became

109

a state. When he was a child, his grandfather used to take him to public executions as a reward for being good. One of his earliest memories was a lynching in Bisbee. "This guy," he said, "was yelling and proclaiming his innocence and all that sort of stuff, and they stretched him from a telephone pole, kicking and hollering. And it developed that he really *was* innocent. They found out later that while we were stringing up this guy, they were stringing up the real murderer in Douglas." As a special treat, his grandfather had taken him to see the first execution of a woman in Arizona. They had front-row seats. Her name was Eva Dubbins, and she'd killed a rancher. She weighed about three hundred pounds. They strapped her into a chair and when she dropped through the trap, her head came off and the blood went all over little nine-year-old Charley Fogarty and his grandfather. He'd met an Indian scout who lived to a ripe old age with a knife tip buried in his head, and a man who'd survived a scalping. He'd watched gunfights in the streets of his hometown. He still spoke Navaho, and talked with some yearning about the sunsets in the Painted Desert.

At age fifteen he dealt with authority pretty much the way he did now. One day in school he got into trouble. So in 1929, he ran away from home:

"The coach took me to be disciplined, and being disciplined meant taking a beating from this big brute. I went into his office. He locked the door and said, 'So you think you're a tough guy? I know how to deal with tough guys.' He went over to the door to get his big stick to give me a beating, and he says, 'All right now, bend over and tie your shoelaces together.' I bent over, but I came up with a hard right and I hit him a real lucky blow on the chin. Knocked him ass over teakettle. I couldn't unlock the door, so I grabbed his chair and broke the glass and ran out the school ground and went downtown. I met this buddy of mine. He was in trouble too. He was just playin' hooky, but he was gonna be expelled. We were both kind of in the same situation.

"There was this freight train that went right through the

110

middle of Tucson. My buddy and I jumped on it and took off and away we went. We got to Colton, California, and lived on handouts, mostly. These brakemen—we called them the yard dicks—chased us. One time they followed us onto the train. The train was really underway and moving, and they were running after us. This guy had a big ol' stick and he was chasing us from the top of one car to another. We leaped from a boxcar to a gondola—or I did—and my buddy didn't make it. He fell in between the cars and just got chopped all to pieces.

"So that was the end of him. I looked down and—I just kinda, I was probably in shock, not so much because of that, but I was alone now. I was all alone and had to do it myself.

"I got to some place, can't remember the name of it. I was skin and bones by this time. I played on sympathy of these old women, for a meal here and there. The Depression was on then. Nobody had anything. I got on a freight train for San Diego.

"I had a .22 revolver, about this big, a little tiny thing. And during the night one of these old bums tried to rape me. I pulled out this gun and I shot him. But I don't know if I hit him. All I know is that he didn't bother me anymore and he didn't move. I got out of there fast—as soon as the boxcar slowed down some. That was the only thing that scared me on the whole trip, these bums, these hobos."

Eventually a freight train took him to San Diego. He went down to the docks:

"I saw this crummy little ship. It was called the *Gryme,* from British Columbia. Wasn't much bigger than a tuna clipper—an old tuna clipper. I walked aboard. I was hungry, hungry as a wolf. This woman—she was the captain's wife, and cook—gave me something to eat. And I signed on as cabin boy. They didn't pay me anything, just food and board. It was a crummy little thing. We went up and down the coast to Vancouver. I don't even know what kind of cargo we had, but it wasn't much.

"I went from one ship to another. They were all coal burners. Didn't have the unions in those days. You made a deal with the captain or the chief mate. It wasn't easy. You had all the overtime you wanted, but you didn't get paid for it. You got forty dollars a month and that's all there was to it. Six men to a room. To wash clothes you had a little bilge, and a plumber's clamp."

Three years later, at eighteen, he missed his ship in Caimanera, Cuba, and found work as a mercenary fighting with Batista against Machado. In 1933, after Batista's victory, he caught a ship out of Havana and worked his way to Norfolk. From there he struck out west by bus, stopping in West Virginia to call on a young woman he wanted to meet, the cousin of a fellow American mercenary in Cuba:

"It was right in the middle of July, and it was hot. I had this address and I went banging on the door. I knocked on the door and here was this beautiful, beautiful girl with blue eyes. I said, 'Is your name Dorothy Cooney?' She said yes. I said, 'Well I'm a friend of Dan Gilbert, your cousin.'

" 'Where is Dan?' she said.

"I said, 'I left him in Cuba. I don't know where he is now.'

"She said, 'The last we heard from him was years ago in Shanghai.'

"She was just a kid, about my age. So she invited me in and fixed me a cool drink and sat down and started talking. We'd been talking about half an hour and I said, 'Why don't you and I get married?' She said, 'Well that's pretty forward.' "

Eventually, she eloped with Fogarty. He took her back to Arizona, where he ran the Navaho reservation trading post in the middle of the Painted Desert.

"She didn't like that at all. She used to watch—the Arizona sunsets are the most beautiful, spectacular things you have witnessed in life. If you've never seen one . . . that was one part of the day my wife liked. She liked the Arizona sunsets. But she couldn't communicate with anybody 'cause she couldn't speak Navaho. She didn't like the coyotes howling and she didn't like the rattlesnakes everywhere. We had 'em in the house, we had

112

'em in the trading post, we had 'em in the warehouse. They were in the barn out back. They were everywhere.

She got used to the Navvies and they liked her. They just sensed that she was friendly. And she *was* friendly. But she couldn't get used to the wind. The wind was always blowing. They had this grass that was about this tall, waist high, sparse, though —blade here, blade there—and the wind would blow it down. It just seemed to blow all the time. She couldn't get used to that. She couldn't get used to the bucks singing all night, a mournful sound, anyhow."

She survived the Painted Desert, and the other places he took her, and forty-seven years later was still married to Charley Fogarty. She'd intervened in his schemes only once, when she caught him making plans to go fight in the Spanish Civil War. "That was one I missed," he said. "I tried to get over there but she said, 'Oh no, you'll get killed and the children will starve to death,' and all this." But he'd managed not to miss World War II, Korea, Vietnam, or even the start of it all in Iran.

May 22, 1819

THE CONVERSATION WAS ABOUT DEATH. IT HAD STARTED WITH THE usual disagreements about the last stitch through the nose. There is a tradition, of obscure provenance, that when a man is sewn up in canvas for burial at sea, the last stitch goes through the nose —to make sure he's dead. Tonight's discussion yielded two more interpretations. Higgin had heard it was so no air would get in and the body would sink. Mr. Flynn had said it was done so the sailor wouldn't be led by the nose on Judgment Day.

This put Cascabel in mind of the moldy seamen's graves in Trinity Church graveyard in lower Manhattan. Someone mentioned Monkey Hill at the old Sailors' Snug Harbor, where over twenty thousand seamen are buried. He said it must be the largest maritime cemetery in the world.

"No," said Higgin. "It isn't."

"What is?"

"You're on it."

Every May 22 there is a little ceremony on the west steps of the Capitol in Washington to commemorate the 5,662 American merchant seamen who were killed during World War II. Congress chose May 22 for Maritime Day because it is the anniversary of one of America's great technological feats: the day in 1819 when the S.S. *Savannah* left her home port of the same name, bound for Liverpool. She became the first steamship to cross the Atlantic.

115

At the Maritime Day ceremonies, taps are sounded, and wreaths are laid. But by now the occasion has become politicized. The merchant marine, while not part of the government, has always been vital to the nation's defense in war time by keeping supplies moving. (The term itself, though it sounds vaguely military, only denotes the country's private, commercial fleet.) Peace time is lean time for the merchant marine. Government contracts are down, and foreign competition has snapped up an astonishing 96.3 percent of the import-export trade, leaving 3.7 percent to American ships. This is, give or take a few tenths, an all-time historical low. It also means the total number of seafaring jobs has dipped to just over twenty thousand.

A great deal of rhetorical energy is spent each Maritime Day assigning the blame for this situation. Management blames the unions for demanding high wages that make the American fleet noncompetitive. The unions blame shipping companies for registering U.S.-owned ships under foreign flags, principally Liberian and Panamanian, to avoid a lot of U.S. taxes as well as high crew wages. (There are about 680 such ships.) And of course everyone blames the government. Both management and labor do agree that the U.S. government should subsidize the merchant fleet much more than it already does.

There are good arguments on both sides, as government task force study groups have shown. Currently, however, no initiatives are under way to correct the problem. It is likely that the American merchant marine will continue to dwindle unless there is another war.

Yet America is so keyed to shipping that the country has gone to war four times because of attacks on her merchant ships. (Against France in 1798, Tripoli in 1801, Britain in 1812, and Germany in 1917.) New England's leadership in the War of Independence had arguably less to do with a tax on tea than the restrictions Parliament imposed in 1768 on Colonial ships—ships that were too successful in competing with the British merchant fleet. Those *were* the good old days. Yankee shipcraft came up with the schooner and the early clippers. By the end of the eighteenth century, American ships carried most of America's trade. The United States was the first nation to establish regular transatlantic passages when the Black Ball Line started packet service between New York and Liverpool in 1816. A century later, the United States had exactly *one* transatlantic line, and her ships were carrying less than ten percent of the nation's trade.

What went wrong in the interim was partly caused by an historical miscalculation. The S.S. *Savannah* did usher in the age of steam, but its technology was better suited to British resources. America lacked coal close to shore, which Britain had in abundance, along with skilled ironworkers. The British government strongly supported its new steamship fleet. Later, the American depression of 1857 and the Civil War caused a sharp decline in shipbuilding. The opening of the western frontier soaked up capital investment and rerouted the national imagination. It wasn't until World War I that the country awoke to find itself virtually dependent on foreign shipping.

There is a story about how, on a congressional junket to the Orient, Sen. Warren G. Harding was leaning on the rail talking to an Englishman when their ship passed a lonely American tramp mid-Pacific. The Englishman laughed and said, "Why would an *American* ship be way out here?" Harding bristled. "And why *shouldn't* it be?" he said.

During World War I America went into a frenzy, building 2,318 vessels, most of which were delivered after the war and were unsuitable for peacetime use. After the war, former Sen. Harding became president, and ordered subsidies to augment the fleet even further. Midwestern congressmen, never big friends of the merchant marine, had most of the subsidies withdrawn.

By 1936, the U.S. merchant fleet was in decidedly bad shape. President Roosevelt, unhappy with the situation, got the Merchant Marine Act of 1936 through Congress by eight votes. A few months later the Maritime Commission awarded the contract for the *America*—the first ocean-going, dry cargo freighter to be built in the United States in fourteen years.

During World War II, Rear Adm. Emory Land, chairman of the U.S. Maritime Commission and War Shipping Administration, and the pharaonic Henry Kaiser oversaw the building of

117

an astonishing number of ships—5,592, merchant and military—during the war. By 1948, nearly sixty percent of U.S. imports and exports were being carried on U.S. ships. But those gravy years did not last long.

Since 1950, the number of U.S. merchant ships has declined by over fifty percent, from 1,224 to 566. In quantity of ships, America now ranks tenth among the world's fleets, just behind West Germany and Italy. Because the trend is toward big ships, however, the total U.S. deadweight tonnage—the carrying capacity—is actually at a record high.

Competition from cheaper, heavily subsidized foreign shipping hurt. So did increased labor costs. An Able-Bodied seaman in the U.S. merchant marine makes about $1,000 per month base pay (with as much as $1,500 or more extra in overtime), and generally works six months a year. A Panamanian AB makes $110 a month, $350 with overtime, and gets three weeks off.

But there is another reason for America's low rank: as in 1819, the country's penchant for high technology has run it afoul of the market. Practically the state-of-the-art ships now afloat are of American design: the container ships, SL-7s, SL-18s, LNGs, OBOs, RO/ROs, LASH ships, VLCCs, and ULCCs. Most of these prototypes came off U.S. drawing boards and were quickly imitated by other countries. But these are highly specialized ships, much less flexible than the old workhorses, and fewer ports can accommodate them.

The *Savannah*, the world's first, only, and probably last, nuclear freighter, a once beautiful, sleek, $41-million masterpiece of technology that could cut water at twenty-three knots, now sits weeping rust alongside a ratty old wharf up river in Charleston. The *Columbianna* was docked next to her before she sailed for Europe. The Japanese did not copy *her* design, sensing something impractical about a cargo ship that needed a bunch of Ph.D.'s to run the engines.

As for her namesake, of the twenty-nine days the S.S. *Savannah* took to cross the Atlantic on her historic voyage in 1819, she was under steam for eight hours.

Things that Go Bump
_____in the Water

TWELVE DAYS OUT OF CHARLESTON, THE *COLUMBIANNA* WAS sixty miles off Brest, France, and heading into the English channel. The sea was calm, and at 2:30 A.M. there was oddly little traffic for one of the world's busiest shipping intersections. It was a clear, cold, starry December night. Young Mr. Darby had the watch. The Captain was below in his cabin, half-conscious of the ball bearings in his ceiling. He had on his powder-blue jumpsuit, which, except for his vanilla-malt-colored jumpsuit, was all he ever wore aboard. He was lying on top of the bed. In crowded shipping lanes he never undressed at night or got under the covers. If Mr. Dexter had been on watch he might have drifted off for an hour, maybe two, before shuddering awake and padding up in his slippers to check the position or peer into the radar cowl through half-shut eyes. But tonight, with Junior on watch, he only dozed, and went up to the bridge every half hour. Junior was how he referred to Mr. Darby.

About 3:30, the Captain checked the course and found it was fifteen degrees off: 052 degrees instead of 037. The Captain asked Mr. Darby why he was trying to put the ship up on French rocks. Mr. Darby explained he had picked up a stationary blip on the radar. It should not have been there, since the chart indicated nothing, but he had assumed it was the oil rig he was able to see through binocs. That would mean the ship was five miles off course, so he had made the fifteen-degree course change. The

119

Captain reminded him of his standing orders to be notified of any course change. Mr. Darby said he hadn't thought it was serious enough to awaken him. The Captain said a fifteen-degree course change qualified as serious.

He went back to his cabin. His gum was bothering him again. He picked up his fifth Louis L'Amour novel of the trip, *The Man from the Broken Hills*. The ocean swell had risen; he could tell from the ball bearings. After five minutes he was trying to keep his eyes open. No reflection on Louis L'Amour.

Toward 5:00, Bob Cascabel, who had the lookout, reported to Second Mate Burke, who had relieved Mr. Darby, that a French naval cruiser was bearing down on her starboard quarter. From one hundred yards a searchlight flicked on, bathing the *Columbianna* in hot light. A Gallic voice came on the VHF radio, informing the Second he had strayed out of the Traffic Separation Zone. The *Columbianna* was too close to shore, out of the shipping lanes entirely. The French have been understandably skittish about big ships coming too close to their shores ever since the *Amoco Cadiz* went up on the rocks and spilled 67 million galllons of crude. The Second Mate thanked the Gallic voice, ordered the helm brought to port thirty degrees, and called the Captain.

At breakfast the Captain told Mr. Darby about being pulled over by the French navy. Mr. Darby flushed red.

"Well," said the Captain, "no real harm done. But you gotta watch it around here." He buttered his toast. "Those rocks'll ruin your whole day."

Mr. Darby mentally reconstructed the episode, but he was stymied. The radar blip had been unmistakable. There was nothing on the chart that should have blipped, except for the oil rig. No buoys, no tidal diamonds. It *had* to have been the oil rig . . . but how could they have gone so far east, completely out of the TSZ? *Shit*, he thought. He stabbed the yolks of his fried eggs. He didn't bother to finish breakfast. Leaving the messhall, he went up to the bridge to go over it again.

The Captain shrugged. "He had some trouble on his last ship," he said. "Some weirdo kept threatenin' him with a paint scraper or somethin'." The Captain finished his coffee. "Whaddya gonna do?"

Three hours later, Sparks took an emergency message from Radio Brest:

CQ DE FEU FFU
MINE SIGHTED 48.27N 05.47W
FFU/1120 GMT/DO/500/487KHZ

This was interesting news. It's not often that forty-year-old German mines come bobbing to the surface.

The Captain looked at the telegram. "Now that *really* woulda ruined our whole day."

The mine's position coincided with the mysterious radar blip. Mr. Darby was vindicated.

Word got around pretty fast, and by lunchtime Slim was telling the story to Gut.

"You tellin' me we almos' hit a *what?*" said Gut.

"A *mine*," said Slim, "a World War II mine."

Gut looked at him uncertainly. "Don't be tellin' me no such thang."

The *Columbianna*'s first view of England had been the *Mayflower*'s last. By 1:00 in the afternoon she was abeam of Start Point. The sun shone brightly. The wind was offshore. She was coasting less than two miles from the ash-colored cliffs that drop hundreds of feet to rocks and surf. The summery greenness of the fields above the cliffs was startling for December, for an area on the same latitude as northern Newfoundland. After a fortnight with the odors of bunker fuel, chthonic plumbing vapors, and human sweat, the pasture smells of dirt and grass that came rolling off the Devon fields were welcome and tantalizing and worked a gaiety on the crew. The Captain and Mr. Fogarty did not complain about each other the entire afternoon. Chiefy appeared on deck, squinting at the shore. Jefferson too. The Ghost seemed especially happy.

She nosed into Torbay, to pick up the Channel-North Sea

pilot, Swindells. He would stay aboard for a week, guiding the ship from here to Bremerhaven and back. He was an amiable, soft-spoken ex-merchant captain in his fifties whose last command had been a three-masted topsail schooner, the *Sir Winston Churchill.* She was a training vessel for maritime cadets, and carried a crew of one hundred and thirty. He'd been her skipper for seven years. Captain Swindells was completely bald, for which he was instantly nicknamed Kojak by the crew. His cheeks and nose were cross-hatched with hundreds of tiny varicose veins. His face was without eyebrows, and had the expressionlessness of an unfinished caricature.

He brought aboard a thick roll of newspapers, which were hungrily consumed by the crew, even the most oblivious of whom were by now slightly curious to see what had gone on in the world. The Captain scanned the *Times, Telegraph,* and *Observer* for stories on developments in the Persian Gulf. Younger crewmen were anxious to know whether Congress had restored the draft. There wasn't anything about that in the British press, but a lot had happened since the ship left Charleston. Headlines told of cozy soirees between the buxom and litigious OPEC divorcée, Soraya Khashoggi, and Winston Churchill, Jr.; of less amorous ones between Mrs. Thatcher and the steel unions; of a fifty-nine-year old grandmother who climbed the Matterhorn; of a hair lotion that turned an eight-year-old into a HUMAN FIREBALL. Rupert Murdoch's *News of the World* was largely taken up that day with the pressing business of Farah Fawcett, Ryan O'Neal, and Lee Majors. The *Daily Mail* had a long piece on the MYSTERY OF THE FLOODING LOOS. The *Daily Mirror* said that Antonio Lopez of Barcelona had been castrated by housewives convinced he had raped one of their daughters; but Mr. Lopez, it developed subsequently, was innocent. And somewhere in the north of England there was a VILLAGE IN TERROR OF ROGUE OWL.

"It's like Broadway," said Mr. Dexter, looking at a night horizon lined with silhouetted ships. "It's like coming down Broadway." The radar showed over fifty vessels within a twelve-mile radius. The VHF buzzed with channel chat.

122

Captain Swindells was in constant motion, plotting loran fixes, taking azimuths on shore lights, looking through the binoculars he never removed from around his neck. He peered into the cowl every two minutes, grease-penciling with an X each new ship that penetrated the radar circumference. Minutes later he would mark another X over the ship's changed position, deducing from the difference the vessel's relative course and speed. The work kept him bent over the screen most of the night. The light given off by the radar's scanner arm playing over his glabrous features, accompanied by beeps and whirs and the clicking of the gyrocompass, gave him the look of a galactic navigator vectoring an approach on some distant nebula.

A few miles off the Isle of Wight he heard a familiar voice on the VHF. It was the first officer of his old sailing ship, the *Sir Winston.* They spoke a while. She was en route to Holland with a crew of women cadets.

"You miss the old girl, Captain?" asked Higgin from the wing deck.

"No," he said. "Not after you've done it for seven years." He went out on the wing deck and aimed his binocs toward Selsey Bill. "I've seen too many funny things that's not funny anymore. I knew a fellow did it for nine years, and he was a bit . . . you know, suffering from delusions of grandeur. You get to be like the Flying Dutchman. *'I will defy the elements.'* Well, you know once you start that it's time to head back in."

"I never sailed on a tall ship, ever," said Higgin. "I'm envious as hell. There was this time once, we were on patrol, waitin' to pick up a unit—quote unquote—comin' outa the Med." He smiled his Cain't-tell-ya-that smile. "We were cruisin' along on a westerly course. I called the Commandin' Officer—I was Junior Officer of the Deck—and told him I had two contacts on my port side, drawing left. And asked permission to come to periscope depth. We were 120 feet. I said to the Dive Officer watch, 'Make the depth 72 feet.' He let me know when we passed 120 feet, 100 feet, then 90 feet, 80 feet. He told the stern planesman, 'Zero bubble. Maintain count at 72 feet.' We came to 72 feet. The scope was comin' out. I spun it around three-sixty degrees several

123

times. I said to the control room, 'No dark shadows. Scope is breaking. Scope is out. No close contacts at low power. Switching to high power.' I searched the horizon. Had one contact. It was a full-rig sailing vessel. She was white hull, white sail, and she was fucking beautiful. A tall ship. God, it was the most miraculous thing," he said. "I just went out of my mind."

At 11:00 that night, the *Columbianna*'s position was exactly zero degrees longitude. This meant Ship's Time was the same as Greenwich Mean Time. On the way over from the United States, the clocks were advanced every three days. The lost hour was divided evenly among the six watches: twelve to four, four to eight, eight to twelve. Each watch was thus shortened by ten minutes.

It was an equitable arrangement, but mathematically beyond the ken of Butts, the twenty-four-year-old AB with the perpetually bloodshot eyes. He hadn't had a drink in almost ten days, but his eyes were still bloodshot.

Even after two weeks he had not got the hang of the time difference and was still showing up for helm and lookout duty ten minutes late. Among seamen there are few breaches of etiquette as unconscionable as being late to relieve your watch partner. Cascabel often relieved Higgin five or ten minutes early. The strong friendship that formed between them began with that courtesy. So by the time Butts lurched through the door to the bridge tonight, *fifteen* minutes late, Pooch was mad as well. Butts, as usual, did not understand why he was late. And this time Pooch did not bother to explain it.

"You're a moron," he told Butts. "You know that, don'tcha? A moron."

Butts said nothing. Later, on the wing deck, staring off in the direction of Omaha Beach, the wind blowing back his long blond beard, he thought it over: "I'm just your basic merchant marine. You gotta explain things to me."

Captain Swindells said there was a Hazard to Navigation Advisory posted: A dead whale had been sighted floating belly up three miles south of Beachy Head. He told the lookouts to watch

124

for it. Hitting a whale can cause surprising havoc on a big ship. At any given moment, men are walking down steep companionways, climbing rigging, leaning against electrical panels, opening furnace doors, pouring caustic liquids, shifting pots of boiling grease. Ever since his nearly fatal collision on the submarine *Ray*, Higgin instinctively cupped his hands underneath the rails to keep from pitching forward in case of a sudden jolt.

Captain Swindells said it wasn't uncommon for whales to turn up dead in the channel, run over by big ships. The *Columbianna* might feel the effects of hitting a whale, but a supertanker wouldn't. Whales that wash up on English shores, incidentally, become property of the sovereign. The law, written in the thirteenth century, gives the head to the king and the tail to the queen. The eighty-five-foot sperm whale that stove in the bows of the Nantucket whaleship *Essex* "with tenfold fury and vengeance in his aspect" on November 20, 1820, and inspired the ending of *Moby Dick* would not have stood a chance against whatever ship had struck and killed the whale now bobbing off Beachy Head. Big ships murder indifferently. Cascabel told of a supertanker that pulled into Yokohama after a trans-pacific run with a yacht's rigging entangled in her anchor. It had gone unnoticed until the pilot boat came alongside and saw the remnant.

St. Leonard's, Hastings, Rye, Dungeness, St. Mary in the Marsh, Folkestone . . . by 0300 she was abeam of Dover and on a course for the German Bight.

Next afternoon the light was dirty yellow through altocumulus translucidus undulatus clouds, the ones that look like uncooked fillets of flounder. There was little wind. A storm was building over Iceland, where the barometer had dropped to 27.9, or 947 millibars. Standard ship's barogram paper, on which a little arm scratches a continuous inky record of barometric pressure, only goes as low as 965 millibars. Captain Swindells was anxious for a weather update. He said the ship would probably be into Bremerhaven before the storm hit, but that coming out would be a "bit of an arsehole."

Around 4:00 P.M. the auto-alarm on Sparks's receiver rang. The alarm is triggered by incoming distress signals, or when the receiver's power drops below ninety amps. Through headphones he listened to the last faint transmissions from a Norwegian fishing boat sinking off Trondheim, six hundred miles to the north. That morning Sparks had received another death notice, from the home office in New York, saying that the chairman of the board of the company had died and requesting that the *Columbianna*'s flag be flown at half-mast for thirty days.

It was midnight, toward the end of Mr. Dexter's watch. Captain Swindells never strayed more than five feet from the radar. Weather and traffic were thickening. A cold wind was blowing down off the North Sea.

Pooch came up the companionway to take his watch at the helm, all scrubbed and ruddy, holding a fresh cup of coffee. "I hear we just about hit a dead whale this morning," he said.

Mr. Dexter laughed at the rumor and went out onto the wing deck. "Uh huh," he muttered, "and pretty soon the wee people will be climbing over the bow." He looked down onto the foredeck and saw a flashlight moving forward toward the number three winch house. It was Slim, with Gut behind him, going forward to smoke a joint.

Nino, the engine utility man, was also smoking a joint. His last one. He wanted to be clean for customs when the ship reached port. Nino shared a focsle with Rocco, an arrangement that had not been working out too well. Having grass in his focsle made Rocco crazy.

Rocco had been simmering the whole way across the Atlantic, complaining that he was going to lose his papers because his roommate was "a junkie." To accommodate him, Nino smoked in the bathroom and sprayed it with Glade afterward. Rocco still wasn't placated, so Nino went on deck to smoke. Even that didn't work. When Nino got back to the focsle, Rocco yelled about how customs would find his dope and bust them both. He said Nino was jeopardizing his whole life. Nino said he didn't have much grass left, and anyway it would all be gone by the time they got to Bremerhaven.

One night Nino was seen on deck at 2:00 A.M., walking aft, draped in blankets like a squaw. He said he was going to sleep in the hospital with the Yansons. Rocco had awoken from his nightmares, he said, and was punching the bulkhead and screaming.

"I tell ya," said Nino, "he's got me shittin' pickles."

There was no room in the hospital, so Nino spent the night curled up on the messhall floor. Three nights later he reappeared in the passageway, covered with bedding, shaking his head. "Fuckin' Rocco," he said. "I feel bad for him, but I don't know what's goin' on. He's wakin' me up at—what time is it?—three fuckin' o'clock in the morning, to tell me the Chief Electrician's on his nerves, and he feels like killin' the Bosun because he didn't like the way he looked at him at the dinner table. Man. . . ."

By now Nino was fed up. He was going to smoke his last joint, in peace—by God—in his bunk, and that was that. Rocco came in, smelled the smoke, and blew up. Nino calmly finished his joint, flushed the roach down the toilet, turned off his light, and went to sleep. An hour later he awoke. Rocco was straddling his chest, pointing the tip of a large screwdriver at his heart.

"One more inch," he hissed, "and it goes in."

Just then Chiefy opened the door, looking for Nino. In a clumsy attempt to get rid of the screwdriver in a hurry, Rocco threw it, missing Chiefy's nose by a foot.

Nino pushed Rocco off his chest, jumped up, and shouted, "Chiefy, you see that?"

"I just saw a screwdriver fly by my nose," said Chiefy. "What the hell is goin' *on* here?"

"Who iss zat—zat *zilly* man?"

The German river pilot—coming on board now that the *Columbianna* was three miles from Bremerhaven—was livid.

Just as he had reached the top of the Jacob's ladder, Pooch took a picture of him. Jumping off a pilot boat onto a rope ladder at night in choppy seas is difficult enough without someone pop-ping a flash in your pupils. (Climbing the ladder is the most dangerous part of a pilot's job. Curiously, if he does fall in, the helmsman immediately steers *into* him, so that the propeller swings away from him.) As the pilot pulled himself, dazed, over the rail, he shouted at Pooch, not finding quite the right words, "You, you, you *embarrass* me!"

Up on the bridge the Captain apologized profusely. The pilot made a rather formal acceptance of the apology, but twenty minutes later was still rubbing his eyes, going, *"Ach, ach!"* to remind everyone that starburst shells continued to fire on his optic nerve.

Captain Swindells was giggling about it on the wing deck, relaxed for the first time in thirty-six hours. With the river pilot aboard, navigation for the time being was no longer his responsibility. But he kept scanning the harbor lights with his binoculars. For pleasure.

He talked about his old ship, the *Sir Winston,* how he had sailed her into Spithead for the Queen's Review during the Silver Jubilee. He said he'd never seen a ship cared for like the H.M.S. *Britannia,* the queen's yacht. Every time the anchor was raised, they repainted it, and seamen who hung over the side with the paintbrushes put white socks over their boots so they wouldn't scuff anything. Captain Swindells was introduced to the queen at a reception. Her Majesty was about to embark on a round-the-world voyage on the *Britannia* and was not at all pleased by the idea.

"I was standing with her, alone for a moment," said the Captain. "You know, *you're* not supposed to start the conversation, so I didn't say anything, but after a bit she said, 'I don't like ships, actually. They're always going up and down and making you feel as though one leg is shorter than the other. They make me seasick.'

"I'm glad I didn't say this to her five hundred years ago, because I probably would've been hanged. But I said, 'Well, ma'am, there's only one sure cure for seasickness.'

" 'Oh?' she said. 'What is it?'

"I said, 'You've got to find a tree and sit under it.'

128

"She looked at me sort of funny and walked away. But I found out later she went over and asked an admiral what the cure for seasickness was. And he starts in with 'Oh, well, ah, ma'am, harum harum, ah, saltine crackers, ma'am, and a spot of tea, dry toast, and no butter—'

" 'No no,' she told him, 'you've got to find a tree and sit under it.' "

There was shouting below as lines were tossed. Tugs were nudging her into a lock. It was cold.

"The medal I'd most like to have," said Captain Swindells, "is the MVO."

"What do you get that for?" someone asked.

"That means you're on, like, *personal* terms with the royal family."

They looked down on the deck and listened to the mooring lines stretching taut. It is an ugly noise, sometimes followed by the sound of men who have just lost their limbs.

"How long ago did you sign off the *Sir Winston*?"

Captain Swindells did not answer right away. He looked to see if they were alone.

"Thursday."

"Thursday?"

"I didn't tell the Captain, you know. I didn't want to make him nervous."

This had been Swindell's first piloting assignment. "I suppose we've all got to start somewhere," he said.

The German river pilot came out on the wing deck. He had just been relieved by the harbor pilot. The scowl and the *ach, ach*-ing were gone. He would soon be home, in bed. He pulled up his collar against the wind.

"Ze vinds are Force Tvelve between Norway and Zcotland," he said.

Captain Swindells nodded.

"Zat ring around ze moon," he said, pointing up at the sky. "Zat is not such a gut sign."

A few minutes after her lines were made fast to the dock in Bremerhaven dock, a sleepy-eyed customs inspector came aboard and rubber-stamped all the forms. The Captain gave him two bottles of scotch. Mr. Darby, as the youngest officer aboard, had to tidy up the bridge. He also made the last entry in the log: "FWE 0248": Finished With Engines, 2:48 A.M. FWE is also written across the files of seamen thrown into foreign jails on drug charges. In either case, it means the voyage is ended. The boilers were cooling. The smokestack was quiet for the first time since the morning up river in Charleston, one million, five hundred twenty-two thousand, and eighty-six turns of the screw ago.

Bremerhaven

CUSTOMS DESCENDED IN FORCE NEXT MORNING, MAKING THE CAP-
tain grumpy. For one thing, he'd already forked over two bottles
of scotch. That's supposed to be the end of the customs formali-
ties. And the foreplay was tiring. He'd been through it so many
times before. The customs man, an old sort with thick glasses, sat
in front of him reading through the ship's stores declaration form,
item by item.

"Two hundred eighty-eight cartons cigarettes?"

"Yup."

"Ten tubes morphia sulphate?"

"Uh hum."

"Nitrostat, one hundred fifty milligrams?"

"Right. What it says. There."

"Yes. Forty gallons kerosene and solvent?"

"Yup."

"*Two* revolvers?"

"Well . . . yeah."

Pause.

"Vhy you have two?"

"Listen, we were in Iran not too long ago. I'll take all I can
get."

Pause.

"Can I offer you a drink or sumpin'?"

"Yes."

They sent a German shepherd to sniff for dope, but she may have had a head cold. No one, except Nino, had been expecting a shakedown. There was dope all over: joints on top of dressers, pipes half full, rolling papers on bunks. Elsa—that was the dog's name—just wagged her tail through it all. Jefferson saw her coming, and ran back to his focsle, and poured an entire bottle of Mr. Clean onto the floor. He was still mopping when she arrived. She sniffed around. He had enough grass in there to keep a small high school stoned for a week but still she didn't seem to notice. Jefferson could not believe this good fortune, and decided Elsa had been trained to signal her handler secretly. That night, he moved his stash to the top of the masthead, expecting a bust. But it never came.

Bob Cascabel said there were ways to beat the dogs. On a ship returning from Chalna, Bangladesh, one of his shipmates had packed away marijuana, hashish, dexedrine, mandrax, cocaine— the whole drugstore. Several days before the ship got into New York, all the pepper disappeared from the shakers. It was a mystery, until it reappeared the morning before the ship was to arrive, sprinkled over every square inch of floor—presumably to confuse the dog's sense of smell. Cascabel persuaded his shipmate to sweep up the pepper and put his dope in the rigging instead. "I've yet to meet the dog," he said, "that could climb ladders."

About half a dozen of the *Columbianna*'s crew had, at one time or another, been caught with dope. Ignacio, the Honduran oiler, had bought an ounce of cocaine mixed with heroin in Bangkok. When his ship hit Hong Kong, which has a reputation for tough customs, he decided on a pretty ingenious hiding place —he taped the stash to the back of the blades of his fan. When customs boarded, one of the agents came to his room. He began searching under the mattress, behind the bed, moving toward the fan. Worried, Ignacio said, "Boy, sure is hot," and turned it on. Centrifugal force and humidity overpowered the gum on the tape, the tip of the baggie edged its way to the fan's wire cage, and whammo: suddenly it was snowing in Ignacio's focsle. Ignacio spent the next eight days in the Hong Kong jail.

The storm that was building between Norway and Scotland dumped chill rain on Bremerhaven during most of the *Columbianna's* stay. The sun shone only once, for a few minutes, like a peeping Tom, then ducked behind storm clouds in the west. At 7:30 the first morning it was still dark. When the crepuscular light begrudgingly diffused itself over the town, it revealed a drab, migrainous skyline. At the dock, two American soldiers had been recently killed driving a tank off a Roll On/Roll Off ship. The steering gear jammed, and the vehicle plunged into the water and sank, turret down. "Lucky fucks," said an AB who had been to Bremerhaven too many times.

The ship's agent, Manfred Klick, arrived later. He and the Captain embraced and asked after each other's families. Their friendship went back to 1968, when Manfred had helped the Captain discharge nine mutinous seamen afraid to sail to Da Nang with a cargo of ammunition. The Tet Offensive was in the headlines those days.

The agent is the ship's liaison to the land. A good ship's agent is a captain's best friend, and can arrange for virtually anything: ship's stores, stevedores, cargo, paperwork. Manfred was a crack agent. He and the Captain made plans over beers.

The disfigured second mate, Burke, was getting off. The bitterness he exuded had been returned. No one talked to him anymore. He had recently complained to the other mates that he could no longer put up with "syphilitic messmen." A new second was being flown in from the States.

The Captain grumbled about the customs hassle. Manfred said he would have a word with the chief inspector, whom he knew well. "A misunderstanding," he said.

The Captain asked what news there was of Iran. The Chief Mate had been spreading rumors about invasion cargo waiting on the dock, and there was an amphibious olive drab thing next to some crates. Manfred said he didn't know what it was and that one of the Shah's nephews had just been assassinated in Paris.

"It is not so lovely in Bandar-e Shahpur this time of year, yes?" said Manfred. "I mean, Bandar *Khomeini.*"

"Whatever," said the Captain.

The action in Bremerhaven, such as it is, is along Lessing-strasse, three blocks of hanky-panky tucked behind a main avenue, where it is less likely to give offense. "By their very vocation," Melville said of sailors, "they are shunned by the better classes of people, and cut off from all access to respectable and improving society . . . the reflecting mind must very soon perceive that the case of sailors, as a class, is not a very promising one." Few of the cabbies that came down to the wharf bothered to ask where their rides wanted to go. It is generally safe to assume a seaman is headed for the worst part of town. But then there is the exception: Higgin, who got into a cab and asked to be taken to the art museum.

"*Vas?*"

"The art museum."

"*Ze art museum?*"

"Yeah. Do you have an art museum here?"

"*Nein nein nein,*" said the driver, who may have thought he was being made fun of.

"Okay," said Higgin. "Seaman's Club."

The United Seaman's Service Club maintains a worldwide network of meeting-places for merchant seamen. They are safe houses. A sign posted prominently outside reads: NO UNESCORTED LADIES ALLOWED. Beer is eighty cents a glass (three dollars on the outside) and the cheeseburgers come without hair. Men can phone home from here, or watch Armed Forces TV. There are pool tables, a reading room, slot machines that pay off, but also make up the deficit the club accrues by keeping its prices low.

Butts was deep into the beers, yet unsatisfied. A few shots of whiskey would do it. He had a fine-tuned sense of his blood chemistry, balancing beer (for bulk) and whiskey (for kick) until the desired level of toxicity had been reached, somewhere between Unconscious and Fatal.

He looked into a window full of whores. They rubbed themselves and cupped their bosoms together and spread their legs apart, moistening their lips and pouting. But after a few minutes they saw he wasn't buying and waved him away with scowls and offended looks. They sometimes managed to make a man feel he was invading their privacy by watching them. Yet here they were, dressed in panties and bras, sitting on high stools behind big glass windows that faced a city street. There were Christmas decorations on the windowsills, little twinkling red lights.

Butts and one of the ABs rounded the corner that had the condom-vending machine, and turned down one of the side alleys going off Lessingstrasse. He'd combed his long blond beard. It looked unnaturally kempt. The booze had sharpened his expression into something like alertness. Halfway down the alley he heard footsteps behind him, and turned. It was a group of Filipino sailors, five or six of them.

"Turn around and face 'em off," Butts whispered.

"Why?"

"It's better that way."

"*What's* better that way?"

"It's always better now than later."

"I don't get it."

"Lissen, I know what I'm doin'."

"Come on."

"Don't worry. I'll take care of you."

"But—"

"Here they come. Get ready."

The Filipinos were on them.

"Hallo," said one of them with a smile and a nod as they passed.

"Jesus," said Butts. "I need a drink."

They ended up at Chico's, a black bar, filled with GIs and seamen. The same movie that was playing at all the other bars was playing here: *Champagne mit Pflaume.* It translates roughly to *Champagne with Pussy* and stars a man, two women, and a stallion. Butts and the AB drew curious, cold looks and were going to leave when J. C. called them over to his table. J. C. was an oiler on the *Columbianna.* He was sitting with Francis, the black chief electrician.

J. C. had stumbled onto Zen when he was a radioman in Vietnam. It was his passion in life. He had first appeared on deck a few days out of Charleston, pouring buckets of furnace slag into the Sargasso sea, wiping his brow and saying, *"The wind blows from the top of Mount Fuji to the Himalayas. Who knows the destiny of my thoughts?"*

J. C. used to say "Zen and languages, that's my life." He'd lived all over the world and knew bits of quite a few languages. The rest he sort of improvised. He talked a nonstop streak of pseudo-German at a cabdriver one night in Bremerhaven on the way back to the ship. The driver looked a bit frightened by J. C. and said nothing the whole time.

"Man," said J. C., getting out, "that guy had *nothin'* to say."

J. C. often told people he was originally from the West Indies, but actually he was from Norfolk. He was an unhappy man, and the reason had to do with a woman.

In 1970, J. C. was discharged from the service in Vietnam after his left eardrum was shattered by a grenade that killed his best army buddy. While recuperating in Saigon, he met a seventeen-year-old Cambodian girl named Con and fell in love. He married her, stayed in Saigon, and got a job with Lockheed. He shaved his head. Con became pregnant. Then one day a telegram arrived from his mother, in Tampa. His grandmother was dying. He knew that if he didn't go his mother would never forgive him. So he left, telling his wife he would be back.

In Tampa, he found his grandmother in surprisingly robust health. The telegram had been a ruse to get him home. On the evening news he saw scenes of an escalating war, heard talk of Cambodia. His family pressured him to stay in Tampa, refused to lend him the money to return. So he wangled a defense contract job with RCA in Greenland. His plan was to get back to Saigon across the top of the world. The ship sailed for Greenland with J. C. and the parts of a tracking station. It hit an iceberg and had to turn back.

He got to Greenland on the next ship and for three months tried to hitchhike a ride on an air transport over the pole to Singapore. He finally arranged it, and was all set to fly out on a Thursday. Wednesday he got a telegram from Tampa: his grandmother was dead, he'd have to go home for the funeral.

136

After the funeral, he joined the merchant marine, thinking he would get to Saigon that way. He caught three successive tramps, all of which were supposed to go to Vietnam. None of them did.

He got off one of these ships and was thrown in jail for drugs. From jail he sent his wife's photograph to a Family Aid agency, which circulated it in the Saigon newspapers along with instructions for her to contact the U.S. embassy immediately. The ad ran for months. Finally a friend of his who was headed back to Vietnam offered to try to track her down. A few weeks later he cabled J. C. she was dead and that the little girl born to her after he left had disappeared.

When J. C. got out of jail, he went back to sea, but he was no longer trying to get someplace.

By now Butts had drunk six whiskeys. Outside, the men ran into some *Columbianna* crew and went to another bar. It wasn't a seaman's place. It was clean and well lit, the waitresses had all their clothes on, and there was no six-foot video screen showing *Champagne mit Pflaume.*

Above the door were three large black-and-white photographs showing downtown Bremerhaven after an Allied bombing raid. Higgin ventured it was there to keep American GIs out, or to make their beer taste bad. Pooch started talking about the time he visited Nagasaki.

Butts was now very drunk. He ripped a twenty deutsche mark bill into little pieces. He put the pieces in a pile and set them on fire. Everyone watched, fairly amazed.

"Why did you do that?" someone asked.

"I done that with a hunnerd dollar bill once," said Butts. "Just *felt* like it." An hour later, he was trying to borrow money, without much success.

Next stop in nighttown was the Bikini Bar. The Third Assistant Engineer was there, clacking his dentures lubriciously at the waitresses. They were wearing come-hither bikinis but go-to-hell looks, so his clacking went unrequited. *Champagne mit Pflaume* was playing on the far wall. No one watched. The two women were running through the forest trying to catch the horse. When they did, it peed on them.

Hooley, a messman from the *Columbianna,* was there, self-conscious about the swastika tattoo on his wrist. He kept it covered. Lukas, a West Indian oiler, was there. Sparks walked in and came over. Pooch talked about the Reeperbahnstrasse in Hamburg. He wouldn't be making it there this trip because he'd drawn day watches that didn't leave time, and he was disappointed. "World famous," said Pooch. "Like a Times Square for sex. Your sadomasochistic sex, your sadist sex, your homosexual sex—whatever sex. Get rolled in this alley, blown in the next alley. World famous as a place for degenerates—which is what we *are,* of course."

Cascabel raised an eyebrow. "Speak," he said, "for yourself."

Cascabel, half Pooch's age, had not yet had the romanticism sucked out of him, but deep down he knew the truth of the matter: "What in your heart do you think of that fellow staggering along the dock. Do you not give him a wide berth, shun him, and account him but little above the brutes that perish? Will you throw open your parlors to him; invite him to dinner? or give him a season ticket to your pew in church? —No." In the more than a hundred and thirty years since Melville wrote those lines in *Redburn,* the seaman's lot has changed dramatically. There was a man on the *Columbianna* who could only with difficulty write his own name, but he had earned enough as an Ordinary seaman to send three children through college. But as a profession, seafaring is not much more respectable now than it was in 1849, when Melville said of sailors, "They are deemed almost the refuse and offscourings of the earth; and the romantic view of them is principally had through romances."

But whatever the world thinks of the breed that staggers along the dock, consider another maritime species, the submariner. Higgin, who had joined the crowd at the Bikini Bar, was not about to let Pooch's remark go unchallenged, so he recited the little ballad he learned in his navy days beneath the surface:

We're lovers, we're fighters,
We're goddam submarine riders.
Smoke, choke, and chew rope;
Dance, prance, and romance.
Make love to men, women, and children,
And various forms of livestock.
Push more peter, more sweeter,
Than any peter pusher.
Hog style, dog style, any style.
No muff too tough,
No thigh too high,
We die for five.
Yea weasel shit,
Fuck!

Next morning was not a happy morning on the *Colum-bianna.* Butts was in great pain, not only from his hangover—he was used to those—but from the puncture wounds in his bottom. He had shoved a cocktail glass in his back pocket as a souvenir, forgetting about it until he'd sat down—collapsed, actually—on the pavement.

Lucas had been rolled, in textbook fashion. His drink was drugged, and he came to without his wallet, his hat, his shoes, or his watch. He had to walk two miles through the snow in stocking feet to reach the ship.

But it was Higgin who hurt the worst. After the Bikini Bar he had gone off with a young lady. They had a go, after which he decided to wash. Drunk and feeling no pain, he filled a sink with near boiling water, dipped his privates in it and left them there for what, to judge from the expression on his face the next three days, must have been much too long.

The Captain too had had a rough night of it and was in his cabin with Manfred, filling out a Not Fit For Duty discharge for Rocco, who was packing his bags to fly home to New York.

The day before, Rocco had gone to see the port doctor, returning a few hours later with a bottle of Valium and a big grin. He swallowed a few, jogged seven miles in the freezing rain, and attacked Nino again with the screwdriver. This time Nino grabbed a fire ax, and they squared off. But the principle of Mutual Assured Destruction kept either of them from making a move. Chief Engineer Muzzio was called. Furious, Chiefy marched them to the Captain's cabin, where the Captain and Sparks were having a quiet drink after a long, hectic day. Chiefy sat Rocco and Nino at opposite ends of the Captain's little round conference table and said this dispute was going to be settled once and for all. Rocco told his side of the story. Nino had started his, when Rocco lunged across the table, ripping Nino's shirt in his frenzy. Nino landed a blow on the side of Rocco's face. The wastebasket was kicked fifteen feet into the Captain's stateroom; Louis L'Amour paperbacks were flung about; crew manifests, stowage plans, customs forms, beer cans littered the floor. Chiefy got Rocco in a headlock—impressive, considering Chiefy's frailty —while the Captain wrestled Nino to the floor. Old Mr. Dexter, going over weather advisories on the bridge, heard the commotion, went down, and thought, *Jeez, this is no good at all.*

The Captain gave Rocco a real chewing out, but didn't log him. He was greatly relieved when Rocco appeared at his door late that night saying he wanted to go home. "These pills, Captain," he said, "they just don't pacify me enough." The Captain listened to Rocco in his fatherly way, and agreed that getting off was *exactly* the right thing to do. Manfred made reservations on a flight to New York.

The Captain was now filling in the blanks on the form under REASONS FOR DISCHARGE and REMARKS. He didn't have the energy to go into detail, so he put down "Emotionally disturbed," and "Recommend more careful screening of personnel."

"If a guy wants to get off," he said, "you let him off. You can open yourself up for a lot of grief if you don't. I'd just as soon not be pullin' screwdrivers outa someone's heart in the middle of the pond."

"Come on," said Manfred. "I buy you lunch, we go to the office and we get away from the ship, okay?" Manfred had recognized the look on the Captain's face. The Russians have a word for it: *tosca.* It means "world-weariness."

They drove north along the Weser estuary to a small

restaurant in Bremen where they ate fresh sole in lemon butter and drank bottles of cold white wine. The Captain relaxed a bit for the first time in a long while, but the talk never strayed far from ship's business. Manfred listened compassionately to woeful tales of Chiefy and the Chief Mate.

"I tell you," said the Captain, pushing his plate away, glowing with Moselle, "it ain't the ships that'll kill ya. It's the psychopaths."

Manfred rolled his eyeballs heavenward in agreement. They reminisced about the mutinous crew of 1968.

"What a time we had then, eh?" Manfred said.

"What a revoltin' development *that* was." The Captain began to laugh, and had to wipe his eyes. This always happened when he laughed.

Manfred told him a story about the captain of another ship. This captain didn't want to be unfaithful to his wife, and never fooled around with whores. Still, he was sometimes away from home as long as a year. He bought himself one of those inflatable dolls and made do with that. One day the ship pulled into Bremerhaven. The captain felt sick, so Manfred sent him to a doctor, who took one look at him and said he had syphilis. The captain told him this was not possible, but a blood test confirmed it. The captain broke down and told the doctor about the inflatable doll. The doctor asked if he . . . *shared* the doll with anyone. Of course not, said the captain. Then did anyone have . . . access to the doll? The captain returned to the ship, and dragged his Bed Room steward to the doctor. A blood test showed that, indeed, the BR had syphilis. Under interrogation by the now enraged captain, the BR confessed to having had quickies on the sly with the inflatable doll.

In Manfred's office, the phones were ringing. One of the ships his agency supplied crews for had gone down in the Sea of Japan the night before. Her name was the *Hatsufuji*. Two bodies had been found; the remaining twenty-two crewmen were presumed dead. "Maybe the captain told the crew not to bother securing the hatches because it was such a short trip, only forty-eight hours," he said. "We're only guessing at this point, it's so early on. The weather got very nasty, and maybe they started taking in water through the hatches." He was standing by a large wall map. On it were two dozen small red magnetic arrows showing the position of each of the agency-staffed ships. An arrow in the Sea of Japan was marked with an H.

"I suppose we can take this down now, yes?" Helmut said, picking it off the map and dropping it into a wastebasket.

Two young men appeared in the mess one morning along with the usual gang of cuckoo clock vendors and duty-free store touts, carrying a briefcase full of watches, bracelets, rings, necklaces, assorted jewelry. They said they were from a Swedish ship that had gone bankrupt in Bremerhaven, and that they were selling their personal effects to raise money to get home. Their story smelled like Limburger, but that only excited the Bosun.

The Bosun was an ornery fellow from Alabama. He'd shot a man. He'd spent time in jail, but not for the shooting—for something else he never mentioned. Most of the crew wished he was still in jail. He was almost impossible to work with. He didn't ask, he screamed—even if all he wanted was a screwdriver or a pair of pliers. His favorite stories involved his screwing people out of what was rightfully theirs. He was thin and mangy, with beady blue eyes, and always had a two-days' growth of beard.

He chose four heavy bracelets, and asked the Swedes how much. Twenty-five hundred dollars. He horse-bargained them for over an hour. It was quite a display of chicanery. By the end of the hour the Swedes were desperate to get away. They said the bracelets were his for fourteen hundred dollars.

"Only *got* seven hunnerd," he lied. A half hour later they were his for seven hundred. He looked awfully happy afterward, thinking he had cheated someone. To celebrate, he got very drunk that night at the Seaman's Club and apparently insulted his cabdriver, because the cabbie backed up as the Bosun opened the door, jamming its edge into his groin. Then the cabbie tried to run over his legs. The Bosun lay howling on the ice. Nino and two others who saw it happen took him to the hospital, where the

Bosun peed all over the operating room, the nurse, and the doctor. The deck crew hoped he would be incapacitated for the return trip, but he disappointed them, as was his habit.

The new second mate arrived, a lean, tall, weathered man, red of neck and with a deep scar running from the left cheekbone across the lips, ending in a puncture at the right side of his jaw. No one asked how he got it but there were the usual speculations. His name was Bodine. He was from Florida and spoke in a Johnny Cash basso profundo.

The last night in Bremerhaven, Bodine sat at the bar of the Seaman's Club. The bargirl was in a foul mood. "You tink you are so vunderful," she was saying to a U.S. Army captain. "Ve did not ask you to come here and protect us. Vhy don't you go avay? You all tink you are so important. I am tired of you."

About ten *Columbianna* men were there, trying to cram in as much predeparture drinking as they could. The sailing board was posted for 0045, meaning everyone was required on the ship two hours earlier, at 10:45 P.M. Bodine was knocking back double shots of Wild Turkey, chasing them with beers. Francis, the black chief electrician, asked Bodine if he could borrow $20. Bodine gave him a look that would have peeled bark off a tree. Francis correctly took it for a no and walked away. Bodine continued his tale of failure at real estate. He had quit the merchant marine after twenty years of sailing and gone into real estate. One year later, with a pretax profit of $380, he went back to sea. He hated the life, but he loved navigation. He loved to shoot the stars. At twilight he'd pace the wing deck, impatient as a gunfighter, waiting for the stars to appear, sextant at the ready in his long arm.

A young German, no more than thirty, sat down on the stool next to Bodine. He was drunk as sin and collapsed onto Bodine's left arm. Bodine glanced at him sideways, and helped him onto his own stool with "A little under the weather, there, huh, pal?" The German raised his highball glass and bellowed, "To Chermany!" In the spirit of the thing, Bodine raised his glass, and said, "Okay, to Germany." The German ordered another double, raised that, and bellowed, "To Helmut Schmidt!"

"Well, I'll drink to that rascal," said Bodine.

The German ordered another, and said, in a kind of hysterical whisper, "To ze S.S.!"

Bodine did not raise his glass. All conversation within a five-foot radius stopped.

"Und Adolph Hitler!"

Bodine gave him a good dose of eyeball. For a moment it looked as though he might coldcock him, but then he raised his glass calmly and in his loud Johnny Cash voice said, "Here's to Jimmy Carter, the best goddam president of the United States we ever had." The radius of stunned silence spread to ten feet. The neo-Nazi went to the bathroom, threw up, and passed out.

"Hey, Bodine," said an Ordinary. "What the fuck you sayin'?"

Bodine leaned over and confided in a low voice, "Personally, I don't think he's a great president. I don't even think he's a good president. But I can't *stand* to hear these damn furners sell our country short." Satisfied, he downed another Wild Turkey and beer, and checked his watch. Nine o'clock. Hell, he thought: plenty of time.

Captain Swindells and the skipper were in the chart room staring at the latest weather report. After several days of waiting for the return leg of the trip, Captain Swindells was anxious to get under way. But the weather report wasn't promising.

2400 HOURS DEC 12

THAMES—DOVER WIGHT	S—SW SEVEN—EIGHT OCCASIONAL SEVERE GALE NINE AND RAIN SHOWERS VIS MODERATE SHOWERS FOG
PORTLAND PLYMOUTH	SW SEVEN TO EIGHT OCCASIONAL SEVERE GALE NINE
BISCAY	SW TO W SIX TO EIGHT OCCASIONAL SEVERE GALE NINE
SOLE	SW TO W LATER EIGHT NINE LOCALLY STORM TEN

Not wonderful. The storm that had followed her into Bremerhaven was now west of Land's End. OTSR had sent in its usual recommendation: via Pentland Firth. "I don't give a shit *what* they tell me," said the Captain, "I ain't goin' through there."

Manfred was below in the Captain's cabin going over the last customs forms. He passed around a small dish of hazelnuts. Sparks took a bite and almost gagged on the condom that popped out of the shell between his teeth. Manfred laughed and laughed. He thought that was just about the funniest thing he had ever seen. Sparks didn't know what to think.

The tugs came alongside. In a few hours Bremerhaven would be astern, a yellow band of fading lights.

Mr. Darby checked her Plimsoll mark with his flashlight. It looked right. Her keel was twenty-seven feet eleven inches beneath the surface. The water came up to the lowest bar, meaning she was properly loaded and ballasted for a winter North Atlantic passage. The Plimsoll mark is painted on the hull of merchant ships. It consists of a circle with a horizontal line drawn through it. Next to that is a vertical line intersected with horizontal bars. The water should come up to one of those bars, depending on the season and the ship's location. In salt water, for instance, which weighs less than fresh water and is therefore more buoyant, a ship can carry more cargo than it can in fresh-water rivers or lakes.

The mark is named for Samuel Plimsoll, a failed nineteenth-century English coal merchant. After his business collapsed, he lived among the poor and became familiar with their hardships, especially those of seamen. In his day, ships were routinely overloaded by unscrupulous owners. Many of them sank. They were known as "coffin ships." Plimsoll was elected to Parliament and campaigned vigorously for a bill to outlaw such overburdening. The debate on the floor of the House of Commons grew so hot that Plimsoll was once moved to call some of his colleagues "villains," and to shake his fist in the Speaker's face. The bill was defeated, but one year later, in 1876, with the tide of public opinion running strongly in favor of reform, the bill was passed as the Merchant Shipping Act. From that time, the mark has

145

been required on all merchant vessels, to show the point beyond which they could not be safely loaded. The *Columbianna's* was partly hidden by umber crumbs of rust and the edges of about thirty coats of paint.

Big Mac, the New York Irish AB, had helm duty. He was semisober, leaning against the wheel to rest his feet, eyes half-shut, waiting for his first order from the harbor pilot. He was alert enough to remember to spin the wheel every few minutes—to relieve the hydraulic pressure that builds up and can jam the steering gear.

Bodine made it up the gangway with visible difficulty at 0030 hours, fifteen minutes before departure. He found his walkie-talkie and took command, so to speak, of the foredeck.

Down in the engine room Chiefy and his men were busy getting up steam. The process takes about four hours. They had increased the flow of water through the tubes running into the boiler, opened the fuel oil valves and the stopcock valve. Now the fuel oil pump was on, transferring fuel from the settling tanks to the ready tanks, from which it would pass through two long pieces of tubing into the burners. Part of the reason Chiefy and the Captain hated each other had to do with the conical fittings at the end of those long tubes.

Nine years ago, in mid-ocean on their first *Columbianna* trip together, the Captain had rung Chiefy on the phone to ask for fifteen nozzles of steam. Chiefy said thirteen would be fine. The Captain said no it wouldn't. Nine years later they were sworn enemies, still arguing about the nozzles.

A nozzle is the orifice through which fuel oil passes to the burner, which then heats the water in the boilers. Thirteen and fifteen refer to the width of the nozzle, fifteen being a smaller width than thirteen. The Captain wanted a size fifteen nozzle because he believed the smaller orifice would allow finer combustion and save fuel.

Chief engineers, not surprisingly, hate to be told their business, and Chiefy was no exception. He preferred thirteen—the wider opening—because it would retard slag buildup. The fuel used on the *Columbianna,* Bunker C, is crude, with a high mineral content of sulphur and vanadium. Crude fuel deposits a lot of slag, and if too much cakes the inside of the nozzle, it can cause blockage, fuel back-up, fuel-pump burn-out. At any rate, it was an old argument, and on this trip, as on all others, Chiefy would be using thirteen nozzles.

When the steam temperature valve hit seven hundred degrees Fahrenheit, the First Assistant Engineer signaled Chiefy. Chiefy rang the bridge to say he had steam. The Captain nodded to the harbor pilot and told the Chief Mate, "Okay, single up, fore 'n aft."

"Single up, fore 'n aft," the Chief said into his walkie-talkie. Mr. Darby aye-ayed him from the stern. Mr. Fogarty waited for word from Bodine up forward.

"Bridge to bow," said the Chief.

Nothing.

"Bridge to bow," the Chief repeated. "Single up, fore 'n aft."

Nothing.

"Bridge to bow." He switched the syntax a bit. "Bow, this is the bridge."

But that didn't work.

"This is the bridge calling the bow."

"Okay," the Captain shouted, "all off."

"Bow, bow, bow," said the Chief, "this–is–the–bridge."

The Chief began to yell into the walkie-talkie, which was very unusual. He never raised his voice. *"Bow!* Is the last line off?"

Finally Bodine's voice came on. "This is the bow."

"Is the last line off?"

"The forward spring is—I—ah—"

"Is the last line off?"

"Right. We'll be ready here shortly."

"BOW! Is the last line off? Is–it–off?"

"We're, ah, gettin' everythin' under control here." Bodine's voice trailed off into static.

"BOW! Get the Bosun and put him on the phone!"

147

The Bosun was below in bed nursing his taxi-mauled groin.
"I think the Second is drunk," said the Chief Mate. Finally
Bodine came on again.
"Last line is off."
"Is it in the water? On the dock? *Where* is it?"
"The last line is off."
"Is it in the water?"
"Coming on board. . . ."

It began to snow. Flakes thick as duck down collected on the
caps of men working in the dark on the foredeck. As she moved
out of the lock and into the Weser River, the wind rose and blew
snow off the gypsyhead. Visibility was about three hundred feet.
The current was running almost six miles an hour out toward
the sea. The current would be with the *Columbianna*, so the
helmsman would have less control. He'd have to compensate for
bow cushion and stern suction.
When a big ship is moving along a riverbank, water is sliced
toward the riverbank by the bow. This increases the volume of
water between the shore and the ship, which forces the ship's bow
out, away from the riverbank. As the bow moves out, releasing the
volume of water between the ship and the riverbank, the escaping
water draws the ship's stern in toward the bank. This is called
stern suction. To compensate, the helmsman will nudge the
wheel into the nearby bank.
There were also a few shoal areas in the Weser, where mud
had silted up mid-channel, making the water shallow. When the
Columbianna's engines were full ahead, her stern would drop one
foot deeper because of the forward thrust of the propeller. This
is called bottom suction. While going over shoalwater, speed is
reduced so that the ship has just enough forward momentum to
maintain steerageway but not so much that her stern digs in too
deep. Ships have been known to bump bump bump their way
across sandbars because captains or pilots didn't lower the speed
enough. Tonight, between the current and the bow cushion and
the stern suction and the bottom suction and the two quarts of

148

warm beer in his stomach, a lot was riding on Big Mac's helmsmanship.

In the galley Yoya was making scrambled eggs and brains for midnight supper. In the engine room, the First Assistant Engineer was at the throttle, turning the wheel according to orders rung on the engine room telegraph: half ahead, dead slow. . . . He could tell where the ship was by the orders he received. He said he had been through the Panama Cana, for instance, so many times he knew the ship's exact position on the forty-mile route by the sequence of the telegraph throttle orders. That was all he knew of the canal. Not once in over two hundred transits had he laid eyes on it.

The foredeck gang set about to stow the mooring lines. It was cold, maybe zero degrees. The lines, heavy and wet from dragging in the water, were freezing up. Tiny icicles forming on the frayed strands of Dacron stabbed and stung. But the lines had to be stowed immediately, because in a few hours, on the open sea, the foredeck would be awash. The snow fell heavily, muffling the sound of the sea.

The Captain sent the Chief Mate forward to take over from Second Mate Bodine. Ordinarily the Bosun would be in charge of anchor watch coming in and out of port. During that critical time the anchor must be ready to drop at a moment's notice in case the boilers lose steam, or the steering gear malfunctions. But the Bosun being out of commission, and Bodine's reaction time not being at its peak, the Captain decided to relieve him. This weather left no margin for error. The Chief Mate told Bodine to have a cup of coffee. Bodine's pride was stung, though, and he stayed by the anchor, smoking, blinking into the snow.

Francis, the chief electrician, appeared on the foredeck. He stood in front of Bodine. Francis was twenty-five, cocky, sober, and shrewd.

"You from Orlando, man?" he said.

"Yeah," said Bodine.

"Man," said Francis, "I *hate* Orlando."

149

Bodine looked at him the way he had at the Seaman's Club. This time Francis didn't walk away.

"Yeah," he said to Francis, "well that ain't my problem." The scar, his height, and the Johnny Cash voice might have scared off a timid man.

"I hate it there," said Francis.

"I said that ain't my problem."

"I couldn't get no pussy there."

"I ain't surprised none."

"What? Pretty little nigger like me?"

Bodine glared.

"I hate it there." Francis stamped his feet to get warm. "Hey, man, how come you so tough? How come you wouldn't lend me twenty dollars like I asked you?"

"Maybe I don't *like* you," said Bodine slowly.

"Oh *man.*" Francis laughed. "That's *good.* Well, I don't like you neither. But I don't think you so tough. I think you pretty soft."

"Why don't you find out?"

"Oh no, man, you the *second officer.* You really big stuff. I'm only the chief electrician. Personally, I think you full of a lot of shit. I know I could beat you bad, but I know better'n to hit the second mate."

Bodine edged over so that his unlit cigarette was an inch from Francis's nose. "I don't like you," he said. "Why don't you try something?"

"I don't think you worth it." Francis laughed again. "You must be a drunk. You pretty *old,* too. I don't get off beating old men."

"I'll show you how old I am," said Bodine, but he made no move.

"Well, you gotta start it, see. I ain't gonna try nothing. But if you start something, I may have to beat you. Might even kill you."

"Maybe *you'll* be dead before this voyage's over."

Francis laughed.

"Why don't you get the hell offa this deck," said Bodine. "You ain't even supposed to be here."

150

"I can be anywhere I want to on this ship. Hell, you *supposed* to be here and you too drunk to do anything."

"I don't like you, you know that?"

"Well I don't like *you*. But I'll light your cigarette. Want me to light your cigarette?" He did. Bodine was caught off-guard.

"Hey," said Francis, pocketing the lighter, "when you get off this ship, you gonna try for your chief mate's license?"

"None of your damn business."

"See? I *told* you you wasn't a nice person. Here I light your cigarette for you and you say something like that. I don't think I'm gonna light your cigarette for you no more."

"I don't give a shit, you know that?"

"See? I *knew* you was a stupid old man. Can't even hold your liquor. Bet you ain't even married. You a drunk, anyway."

"Know what you are?"

"What's that?"

"You're a nigger."

"What you calling me your family names for?"

"Why don't you get the hell out of here?"

"I was going to, but then you called me a nigger. Know what I'm gonna do?"

"What?"

"I'm gonna ride your ass this whole trip. Every time you fuck up, I'm gonna be right there."

Bodine stiffened. He had five inches on Francis. His hands balled into fists and his lips went thin. But a fight would have been over in three seconds. He could see that, even through the fog of his hatred. He pressed his face toward Francis's.

"You're just a nigger."

"Hey man, your mother must not be a nice lady if she taught you to speak like that."

Lucky timing kept the fight from going any further. The Chief Mate passed by them. Bodine swerved:

"Chief, this nigger—"

"*Hey,* man," said Francis, "that ain't nice."

"You shut up. Chief, this nigger won't get off the deck."

"Come on, come on, come on," said the Chief Mate wearily.

151

He asked Francis to check the fuses on the cluster lights. The fuse box was a hundred and fifty feet away. Francis smiled.

"Sure thing, Chief," he said, and disappeared into the blizzard, hands holstered, leaving Bodine standing alone by the gypsy-head, while the rest of the men on the foredeck finished with the lines, went to the galley for coffee, scrambled eggs, and brains.

Cascabel

IT WAS BELOW FREEZING, THE SUN WAS A SMEAR OF DIRTY LIGHT over Schleswig-Holstein, the swells out of the north were fifteen feet high and nauseous, and the barograph paper looked like a Dow Jones report in October '29. Still, all this was preferable to waking up in Bremerhaven.

Sparks had achieved just the right atmosphere in his radio room: one part smoke to four parts air. He was trying to get a long-range weather forecast from Norfolk. Norfolk had sent him the advisory for November 12; he had cabled back that this was December 12; they had again sent the one for November 12. The third time they got it right. Total cost of telegram traffic: about two hundred fifty dollars. What they reported was a Force Nine "Strong Gale" moving over the Pentland Firth, and a Force Ten-plus "Storm" off Brittany. The Captain dimpled one cheek in disgust.

"They got 954 [millibars] up there," he said. "That's 28.21 [inches]."

"That's pretty low, huh?"

"That's a real bearcat is what that is."

Captain Swindells had the bridge to himself. He was glad to be working. He'd heard over the VHF that it was "pissing" in Dorset, and he worried about his wife and five-year-old daughter.

Cascabel had the wheel. "Do you know what Goethe said about Germans?" he asked. Captain Swindells said he did not.

153

" 'Never have I seen a people more estimable in their singu-
larity and more wretched in their generality.' "

Captain Swindells laughed. "Oh yes," he said, "I like that."

Robert Cascabel was raised in New York City, the son of an
NYPD Homicide detective. He last saw his father seventeen years
ago. The detective in the family is his mother, a very attractive
woman with an impressive record.

His grandfather was a Maltese sea captain who was awarded
the Victoria Cross during World War I for his ability to talk
cornered German submarine captains into surrendering.

Cascabel put himself through New York University by working full time. Once he ran out of money. His pride prevented him
from asking his mother for help, so for two weeks he subsisted on
a case of Major Grey's East India Chutney—foisted on him by
a worried friend—and tea. His weight dropped from its customary
230 pounds to 180. When his paycheck finally arrived, he hopped
on a train and went to Washington, D.C., to see an exhibition
of Leonardo da Vinci's sketches. He is given to such impulses, and
one day the impulse seized him to go to sea:

"We went to Bangladesh on my first ship, to Chalna. An
amazing place. We dropped the hook [anchor] in the afternoon,
late afternoon, about four o'clock. They hadn't broken watches
yet. We were afraid of people stealing our mooring lines—a very
thriving business in Bangladesh. Mooring lines are expensive. Ask
the Captain how much a mooring line costs. A lousy shackle, a
tempered steel shackle, costs forty dollars. Thriving business in
Chalna and in the Philippines and a lot of other places. So we
dropped the hook, and the Mate tells us that he wants three of
us on watch, one on the bow, one on the stern, and one person
midships on standby in the messhall, by the phone. I was up on
the bow, my watch partner was on the stern, the other one's in
the messhall, and we all had whistles. In case anything should
come up we'd blow our whistle.

"So I hear this whistling like mad back on the stern and
thought, oh oh, something's happened. I didn't know what the

154

hell it was, so I go running back aft. I've got an anchor hook, it looks like a big longshoreman's hook, and my watch partner back there's got a lead pipe. And I didn't know what Frank had, but I go running back there and there's about maybe five or six grappling hooks wrapped in rags and lines hanging off them, and there are guys climbing up the lines. And there were a lot of little boats right underneath the stern where you can't see them unless you really bend under to look. And these guys are climbing, they've got the ropes between their toes and they're climbing up the lines and there's about four or five of them on deck. I see Harvey back there swinging his pipe like mad, going crazy with his pipe, and I come back there and the excitement was incredible. All my life I've waited for something like this. Really. *Pirates.* I had my anchor hook and I just let out an incredible yell and started swinging this anchor hook over the top of my head and I guess I must've scared them. And there were a lot of 'em there. They were right in the middle of throwing all the oil drums over the side. They were stealing all our oil drums, the fifty-five-gallon drums. All I hear was ta-*dum*, ta-*dum*. Harvey was yelling and screaming with this pipe over his head. You know, all sorts of abuse and whatever dirty names you can think of, he's yelling and screaming.

"Well, he was *trying* to attack them but Harvey was big and slow and these guys were really small and fast, and one of 'em had cut him on the shoulder with these big banana knives. It wasn't anything serious. It didn't do anything but make Harvey mad. Harvey liked to put up a very bold front, but I knew inside he was a marshmallow, and he didn't know what to do except yell and hope he could frighten them away with his size.

"The outcome was, Bengali pirates got eight barrels. Crew of the *Jeff Davis,* nothing. All we managed to do was to scare them off but they got all the barrels.

"They went after the garbage barrels, anything. Anything that wasn't nailed down. Had the extra mooring lines not been secured they probably would've tried taking the mooring lines, but they were well secured, and we were going to put them down into the line locker anyway. But they got a lot of barrels. I don't know what else they got. It was crazy. That night I went into town, if you want to call it that, and my boatman said to me— we were rowing up river—he said, 'If you see boat, one come on this side, one come on that side, that means we must fight. But do not worry for I shall fight *with* you.' Which gave me an awful lot of . . . made me feel very secure, you know, that you're liable to be attacked in the river by pirates. Tigers and snakes and all kinds of things. Glorious town. I have to go back.

"All the old-timers talk about Chalna and they all go *yuch*, but I love it. A lot of guys, the older guys, I guess after awhile you become kind of bored and jaded and you really—you really don't care, you're just out here for the money. But I get to do things out here that I wouldn't be able to do anywhere else. I think it kind of suits my personality, the way I am, because I'm a romantic. I'm one of the few people I know that fences rapier and dagger.

"Legacy, perhaps. I'm the son of a son of a sailor [on both sides]. Even my great-great-grandfather, according to my grandfather, was a Captain. He was Maltese. Everybody, Venetians, Greeks, Romans, Carthaginians—they all conquered Malta. The Germans were the only ones who didn't. But everybody who has ever had more than five ships has taken over Malta at one time or another. They would defend it at incredible loss until finally it had to fall. That's the blood that goes through my veins, and sometimes I think about that.

"The adjustment coming home was very difficult for me. I'd been gone for almost a year. And I didn't realize how much it changed me. I'd seen a man killed, I'd saved a man's life, my watch partner had a heart attack right on the deck. I'd almost been put in irons by this crazed third mate. And to try and tell people, to explain how something affects you emotionally is a difficult thing to do, and I'm not very good with words. To try and tell somebody about two little beggars that live on the dock on Bangladesh, one with no arms and one with no legs, and the amazing ways they would work together just to keep each other alive. The one with no legs would feed the one with no arms, and

156

the one with no arms would carry the one with no legs around. They had it down to a system, and were perfectly adapted, it was a perfect example of symbiotic living. One could not survive without the other. It was hard to talk about that in Long Island. You have to see it. It's something you have to see. The snake eater of Cochin, for instance.

"We were in Cochin, India, and I was working on deck. There were all kinds of bumboats [native boats] on the starboard side. We were tied up port side. And they were down there sellin' things, little carved wooden boxes, and there was one guy that had a little girl beating a drum and an old man who rowed, while the guy sat in the stern. What he did for a living is you'd give him a rupee or couple rupees. He'd wait till there was a crowd, and he collected some money from everybody. He had a big plastic jar and the jar was filled with water, and inside the jar were two snakes: one snake about a foot long, and another snake about a foot and a half long. What he would do is take this jar of water and swallow the entire thing, must've been over a gallon, and swallow both snakes. And the snakes would come up through his esophagus. One of them kind of came up through his nose, he stuck its head out of his nose, just looked around—you could see the tongue coming out—and he drew the snake out of his nose and put it into the jar. The other one came out of the same nostril. It was about as thick as a silver dollar is across. Things kept happening on that trip.

"A few guys in the deck department were stoned by a crowd of Bengali children. I don't know what the reason was. They had been drinking in a bar and they went and drove around in a cab somewhere, and as they got out these children just started pelting them, pelting them with large stones, as if they were trying to kill them.

"One of these guys later turned into a Jesus freak, and another one, one who had been a Jesus freak all along, well—he was a saloon messman and he was always talking about Jesus. First couple weeks he was out on the gangway every night trying to convert the Moslem watchmen to Christianity. The Moslem watchmen ended up converting *him* instead, and after a couple weeks, he started going to the opium dens. Well, he wound up with syphilis and gonorrhea *and* the crabs.

"He would read out of his Koran every morning, diseased, in the hospital, wrapped up in a bathrobe. With his *kufi* and his Koran, reading and rocking back and forth. This is what Chalna can do to you if you don't have the constitution for it.

"I later met his brother. I asked him what happened to him. He told me, 'We figured to send him to sea so he might straighten out. Boy, were we wrong. He left as a fundamental Christian, which we couldn't stand; he came back as a devout Moslem with syphilis, gonorrhea, and the crabs—which we liked even less, not to mention his new opium habit.'

"God, I'm feeling left out. Everybody I know is getting their master's degrees now and I've got nothing to show for it. It still impresses them when they ask me how much money I make. They don't realize just what you've got to do for it though. I don't know. Sometimes I have second thoughts about it. I think, well to hell with it all. Because I feel that I do miss an awful lot, as far as what happens on the beach. And I am very much out of touch; I don't like that.

"Some people put up with it out here and others can't. Some people that just can't cut it anywhere else. Seriously. There are people who just would not be able to hold down a nine to five on the beach. I've done it for awhile, but I didn't like it. I really despised it. I can't really say it was the routine, because I have a routine here. But I have more freedom here. I have more personal freedom, within the system, than I have on the beach. The whole key to freedom is to know your limitations, and to know just how far you go. Once you know the game and you know the rules, you're free. Because you can navigate through the forest of all those rules and all those little things that stand in your way and make it difficult for you. Once you know where the trees are, it's not very difficult to get through the forest. I know where all the trees are out here, but on the beach somebody's always putting a new one right in your way.

"I like it here. I like what I do, and I feel I do what I do fairly well. And I enjoy being good at what I do, it's an important thing for me to be good at what I do. There's a craft to it. It's like joining the Masons or something. Really, it's a very closed community where everybody knows everybody else and you do build up a reputation for what you do, and I like that. I enjoy it. I have to say I've learned a lot from other people, but also a lot of it myself. Nobody, but nobody, is born with a wheel in one hand and a marlinspike in the other. Everybody has to learn somewhere. You learn by watching, by doing, by asking questions. And if you don't know, you shouldn't be ashamed to say 'I don't know, show me.' That's the most important thing. So many people are really ashamed and will not admit if they don't know something. And I find my shame in that. This third mate, the new one [Mr. Darby], you know what he did last night? He doesn't want anybody to know about it but I know about it, and I've gotta give him credit for it. We were on auto[matic pilot] and he took it off auto and he steered for awhile—simply because he doesn't know how to steer and he thinks that he should know. And he *should* know. But it takes a little bit of balls to do that, to get an Ordinary to teach the third mate how to steer.

"What I like about the Bosun—well, I hate *working* for the Bosun, I really hate working for him, he's a pain in the ass to work for—but he's all right to sit down and have a drink with and he'll make coins disappear and all those tricks he has. He'll keep you laughing. But I respect him a helluva lot more than I respect the Second Mate.

"You know, a few days ago the Bosun and that messman were comparing school illiteracy stories? Trying to see who could get the best on who: 'Well, I only made it through the second grade.' 'Well, I made it through the third grade but only *barely.*' 'Can you read?' 'Well, yeah, well sometimes. But I can't pronounce all the words.' And I'm sitting there watching them thinking, *My God, neither of these guys can read.* And this is the United States of America in the twentieth century. He screams and shouts a helluva lot, but he's good in his job. He's just a little too overtime hungry for me. Higgin's theory is that the reason he may be yelling all the time is that he may have hurt someone in

159

the past. He may have hurt somebody or he may have seen somebody seriously hurt and so he yells. Anybody that's been out here for any period of time is gonna see somebody get hurt.

"It's so easy to get hurt here. It really is. I've seen wires snap and lines part and all those kinds of things and, well, thank God nobody's been hurt on this trip, but I've heard the horror stories and I don't want to be one of them. I've come so close on several occasions. Once the only thing that saved my life was the fact that I was loafing, which is something I don't do that often, but I was just mad. It was on the *Pittsburgh*, a Sea-Land ship. I couldn't stand the bosun and I was on gangway and he wanted me to go up and tighten up the lines up on the bow. I was all mad. He told me to go do it right away. He was up there and another AB was up there, and I took a damn time getting up there, I really did.

"This AB was taking up on a line, this nylon line. Nylon line will stretch to thirty-three percent of its length before it'll snap, and then when it snaps it's like a rubber band, it'll come back at incredible speed. A manila line or a wire will pretty much hold together when it parts, but a nylon line will explode into a thousand little whips. Thousands of little strands, and any one of them can cut you in half. It was a brand new line, a tug line, which was a little bit heavier than the other lines, and they had it on the bit, and they were taking up on it. The line took an incredible strain just as I was coming up to where I should have been, flaking down the line [laying it out on deck]. The line parted and just snapped back about sixty feet, wiped out a life ring, just tore it to shreds. There was no piece bigger than my fist, and it tore the hell out of a rail and the stand, the little box that the life ring goes in, and it cut the rail up into about three pieces. I would've been right in the way of that line had I been doing my job. I would've caught it. Sure as shit I would've caught it. And it makes you think.

"The scars you see . . . one guy on the *Jeff Davis* had one pretty vicious looking. From right below the sternum all the way down to the groin, with cross trees on it, stitch marks. He was stabbed by the captain of a tugboat down in Houston. We have one guy on board, Pooch, who doesn't have a belly button. There is something about all of this that somehow people on shore don't want to listen to or don't understand. I think it's they don't want to listen to it. People were a little more open to the snake man of Cochin because they want to believe that thing about *those* people.

"Seamen in general have seen so many outrageous things, and things that nobody else really gets a chance to see. I mean you can tell something to seamen and they will believe you, because they've got stories, things that they've seen that no one but other seamen will believe. I never would have met Roger if I hadn't gone to sea.

"Roger was Ethiopian. He was young, he was about twenty-six, twenty-seven. And he was working on his master's at NYU. I guess it was '76, '77, around there. I had been in the same area at the time, but hadn't met him there. He only lived a couple blocks away from where I lived. We used to frequent the same bar—Mcsorley's Ale House.

"Roger's family was very well off. A merchant family. They were doing quite well. His father and his uncles were all in business together. It was exporting—something to do with cloth, I don't remember. When Haile Selassie [emperor of Ethiopia] was killed and the insurgents took over the country, his family kind of got into some trouble. He interrupted his classes and went back more or less to check up on his family and make sure everything was all right. He was going to go back to the United States and finish his education. He almost had his master's degree in economics.

"At home, he found out his father and, I believe, two of his uncles were killed by the rebels and there was nobody really left to support the family. So he was elected; he had to support his family. The Ethiopian rebels, you know, they had an educated man here, he's almost got a master's degree in economics, and they got him a job. They wouldn't let him leave the country, wouldn't let him return, and he had to support his family besides. So they made him the boss in charge of the longshoremen on a ship, which is supposed to be a good job for a man with a master's degree in economics. And that's where I got to meet him, in Assab, Ethiopia. I was on the *Jeff Davis.*

"We weren't allowed to go ashore because there were a lot of Russian vessels in the port. Cuban troops, Russian vessels. We were carrying a load of farm machinery to them, it was all government giveaway. U.S. government, hand-shake stuff. They were afraid of fights and what have you. So we were restricted to the ship under orders of the government. But I met him, and I got to talk to him, and I found out all these incredible coincidences: that I lived on Seventh Street while he was living on Sixth Street, that we used to go to the same bars at about the same time. He was very soft-spoken. He spoke excellent English. Very, very intelligent man. He could see through the bullshit. He knew what was going on. And he was an interesting person to talk to. I liked him a hell of a lot. I would have liked to have known him more.

"We were there for about three days. His job was pretty much just to stand around and make sure nobody was screwing off and that cargo was handled correctly and nothing got busted up. He was timekeeper and—oh God, everything else. He was the Man in Charge. He'd bring me coins, the old silver coins with Haile Selassie on them. I still have some at home.

"We finished loading. He had mentioned a couple days before we finished how much he wanted to get back to the United States and finish his education. We realized that his position in that country really was kind of untenable. He had to support his family, yet he had to think for himself. His family had some money and they would be pretty well off. He wouldn't have to worry about them too much. All those that had offended the new government were gone anyway. It was just him. And he knew sooner or later they were going to get on to him, so he felt he had to leave: he had no choice. And we left. And that was the last I saw of him . . . for about two or three days, when I heard some rattling around in the forepeak. I went down there—and who in hell should be down there but Roger, hiding up in the forepeak. And I thought, *Oh oh.* I'd heard about stowaways but this was the first time I'd seen one. And I didn't know what to do, so I did nothing. I brought him food and water that could get me in a lot of trouble if they found out.

"Now I'm trying to maintain this big secret. Here I am supporting this man, bringing him a liter bottle of water everyday, and then I found out he had *two* liter bottles. I didn't know where the other one came from. I found out almost everybody in the crew knew about him and everybody was bringing him food. He'd probably never eaten so well in his entire life. If you didn't mind the smell in the forepeak. . . .

"So he was sitting in there. I think I'd only been in there once and I was on that vessel for seven months, so it was a pretty out of the way place, and he was just hiding out in there. Everybody knew about it. Everybody liked the guy, because he was intelligent and he was not one of them. He spoke English and he was courteous and he expected courtesy in return, and you treated the man with an amount of respect. And what happened was one loudmouth son of a bitch just went up and brought the whole thing out into the open. I'm sure the Captain and the Mate knew about it, or if they didn't know I'm sure they had an idea. But once it was out in the open and it was officially in the book that a stowaway had been discovered, there was really nothing they could do.

"They took him out of the forepeak and kept him in the hospital where he at least got to shower and use proper sanitary facilities, and have decent meals and everything. He had pretty much freedom of the ship because really there's no place to go. But when we hit port—Madras, Cochin, Colombo—he was restricted to the hospital. He was kept locked in the hospital.

"Well, it was kind of obvious what we had to do. We had to return him to where we got him from. Which is what we did. We were going to be passing by on the way back through the Red Sea. Terribly close. Really not very far, just a few hours, maybe six hours out of our way.

"When we'd left Assab the first time, they had sent soldiers on board to search for stowaways. I'd never seen a pair of soldiers like these. They were both about seventeen years old. One was all dressed in green fatigues—I mean, from his green fatigue sneakers up to his green fatigue baseball cap with a little red Communist emblem on top. Over his fatigue shirt he had this blue polo shirt on with a photograph of a couple kissing on it, and I thought, *Boy, this is strange.* But from what I understand they always search outbound ships for stowaways.

"On the way back we turned him over to the customs agents and Cuban soldiers. I think they were Cuban soldiers—I couldn't tell. And we put him in the launch. I got to talk to him before he left. I was standing by the gangplank and I wished him luck and . . . and he wished me luck and . . . we talked about Mcsorley's Ale House in Manhattan. That was one of the last things we talked about. And the launch came alongside. He said, 'You know what I was thinking about? I was thinking about Mcsorley's and the man carrying all the pitchers of beer.' And I had been thinking about it too, and wondering if I had seen him or not, and I said, 'Well, I was thinking about it the other night also.' And I told him it was a shame I'd never met him before, because I would have liked to talk to him a little more. Then I asked him, 'What do you think will happen?' He said, 'They'll probably kill me.' And at first I really didn't believe him, but the more I thought about it I thought, *Yeah, they probably* will *kill him*. It seemed, you know, it seems that's the way that things go, that's the way they happen. It's a country in an area where life is just very cheap. Rather than put somebody in prison it's easier to just put a bullet in him.

"They came and they took him into the launch. Put handcuffs on him. And he almost fell down the gangway—he had his hands cuffed behind his back. They brought the launch up to the dock and marched him off toward the beach area and stood him up near the water and they just shot him to death. I saw it. There was nothing to do. I had expected it. I guess I was prepared for it—as prepared as you can be, you know.

"I grew up on the water. I knew it was always there. Rather than being a boundary, it was a highway. That little stretch of water just out front, you can just get on that and go anywhere, anywhere. The water was—the sea was never something that kept me in, it was always something to get me somewhere else. But it makes you very cynical. Yeah, something I've been fighting. I don't want to become cynical, but it does make me cynical. That's what Fred, my best friend, told me when I came back. He said, 'You've gotten very cynical.' "

Weevils

I find the sea life an acquired taste, like that for tomatoes and olives. The cold, motion, noise, and odor are not to be dispensed with.

Ralph Waldo Emerson
English Traits

THE MORNING AFTER THE *COLUMBIANNA* PULLED OUT OF BREmerhaven, Bodine arrived for his watch looking awful. A paperback copy of *Advise and Consent* jutted from his back pocket. His hands were shaking and he kept complaining about how he couldn't shoot the sun—that is, take a sextant fix—through the cloud cover. He was desperate to shoot *something*. After two hours of coffee, nicotine, salt air, radar vectors, and dead reckoning he improved. He didn't remember much of last night's fight with Francis.

But Francis did. He asked Higgin to give Bodine a message. Higgin said sure, what?

"Tell him I'm gonna fuck him up *bad*," said Francis. "I'm gonna come up there every morning and ride his ass."

"*Hey,*" said Higgin, "I don't deliver hate mail. I believe in eye-to-eye contact."

"He called me a nigger."

"Well," said Higgin, "I guess there are bigots."

Francis nodded. He knew all about bigots.

"I had this friend," said Francis. "He was white. We was always hanging around together. If you saw him, you saw me. We was *in*-separable. But his daddy didn't like that. His daddy was a merchant seaman. So one day we was hanging around and his daddy starts talking to me in this really friendly tone of voice, which was strange, 'cause he had never liked me. Never. 'Cause I was black. And he says, 'Whatchya gonna do with your life?' I said, 'I don't know.' He said, 'Well, why doncha go to sea?' I said, 'Well, that don't sound too bad.' He called up this friend of his in the SIU and fixed it up.

"I went home to my momma and said, 'Hey, momma, I'm goin' to sea!' She said, 'Why you wanna be a bum?' "

Francis laughed.

"That's what she thought of *that.* But I went. And I come back a couple of months later and I go see Robert [his friend] and now *he* wants to go to sea—which give his daddy a *big* pain in the ass. Merchant seamen don't want their *own* sons goin' to sea. But now Robert wants to go to sea—and the reason is I been writing him and telling him about the shit I been doing, the places and the women and the life. Like, it *can* be a good life. But now I hate it. I been here nine years. Anyway, Robert never made it to sea. They moved to England real suddenly after that, and I never seen him since. I'm sad about it. Now I'm trying to get out of this.

"I had a job ashore a couple of times. I was making five bucks an hour, and out here I make twice that, easy. Five hundred a month—clear. Plus I got my vacation and my room and board. But I want to have my own electric business. I need a van. I need to pay off my debts—I didn't make no money last trip cause of that Bosun's poker game. I ain't gonna tell my wife about that, though. Thing about home is, every night you come home. And I can't hack Beazely's clothes bills [his son, age six]. My wife's telling me he got to go to school in a three-piece suit, that kind of stuff. I say, '*What?*' When I went to school I'm wearing cut up Adidas and blue jeans that's more cut up. On the beach, I just

166

don't seem to make any money. I'm always broke. But I'm going to get out of this, see."

Late in the afternoon, Slim and Gut and some others went down to Dogbreath's focsle. Dogbreath—it was a pretty accurate nickname—was one of the young engine room oilers. He had bought some Turkish hash in Bremerhaven, strong stuff.

The ship was taking twenty-degree rolls. The motion reminded someone of a book, *Death Ship*, by B. Traven. It was about a doomed frieghter cruising these same waters. Dogbreath said not to spread it around, but coming out of the harbor last night one of the boilers almost exploded.

"*What?*" said Gut.

A diaphragm blew, Dogbreath said, the ship lost power, and the steam pressure shot up past the red mark.

He tore off another piece of wafer-thin hash and braised it with the lighter. "Shoulda seen Chiefy. Thought he'd lost it. Man, he was a nutbasket."

"Wait a minute, wait a minute, wait a minute," said Slim. "He's talkin' 'bout some death ship, an' now you sayin' we almost blew up last night?" He looked at Gut.

Gut said, "Everybody else talkin' about this storm we headin' into. Everybody sayin' it's gonna be a *bad* muthafucker."

"Good gracious," said Slim.

Dogbreath produced a thick wad of Polaroids—pictures of his girl friends. He had girl friends everywhere. Dogbreath was blue-eyed and handsome and kept in shape. Before he went ashore prowling for girls, he used a lot of mouthwash. Some of the girls in the Polaroids were naked. Slim and Gut flipped through them as Dogbreath explained where the girls were from and what they did and how good they were and how many times they could do it. There was one, a stewardess from Panama City, Florida, lying on top of a bed, smiling. The skin around her vagina was noticeably red, even at ten feet. Gut approved.

"He took this one after he fuck her," said Gut. "Maan, look like a *stab* wound."

167

Chiefy was in a foul mood. He took the blown diaphragm as he did all mechanical breakdowns—personally. Two days ago at the Seaman's Club he'd been talking about "my great crew down there." Now the First Assistant was a "stupid idiot," the Third Assistant a "dumb asshole." When he arrived in the mess-hall tonight he announced, loud enough to make sure the Captain heard, "Nine years on this cocksucker—I'm goin' to diesel!"

Chiefy was no longer sitting at the Captain's table. On his own initiative he had moved to the engine room officers' table, where he held beggar's court.

The Captain was certain Chiefy had not taken on enough bunker fuel in Bremerhaven. And Chiefy had never divulged how much fuel was aboard.

"He told me he's got fifteen hundred barrels up his sleeve," said the Captain, eyes pinned on his ice cream. "I guess I should consider myself fortunate he's got that much." The Captain was also eating Oreos. Before putting each one in his mouth, he tapped it, edges down, on the table.

"What're you doing, Skipper?"

"Tappin' out the weevils."

"The *weevils?*"

"Yeah."

"Oh."

"You mean all this time you been on ships you never tapped your cookies?"

"No, sir."

"Well then you've et a lotta weevils."

By midnight she was off Dover. The wind was blowing hard, about forty. The night was cold and starless; tenebrous. Casabel put his head through the porthole and let the rushing air scrub his face while he watched what he thought must be the Dover-to-Calais ferry laboring into the chop.

He pulled his head inside and sat down, face hot with wind-burn. He felt emptiness, loneliness. The Mint Frappe walls stared at him insolently. He lit a Camel and looked out the porthole, toward Dover Beach and the edge of the darkling plain, and listened to what Matthew Arnold had heard, a

> *melancholy, long, withdrawing roar,*
> *Retreating, to the breath*
> *Of the night-wind, down the vast edges drear*
> *And naked shingles of the world.*

Most of the crew was in the messhalls watching *Last Tango in Paris.* He thought of going to the radio room and listening to the VHF traffic. When he felt depressed this way there was comfort in the precision of electronic sounds. . . . *Affirmative, Kilo Papa, switching to eight.* . . .

He was about to leave when Pooch stuck his head in on the way down from the bridge. "Hear that hum?" Pooch said. The superstructure was humming. "Listen. Lower than the generator hum. Hear it?" It was the wind. "That means it's over fifty [knots]. They're sayin' Force Ten by tomorrow night." Then Big Mac stuck his head in on the way up. Cascabel looked at the huge ex-chief gunner's mate. Big Mac was drunk again. His nose was livid with varicose veins, in contrast to the bloodless lower lip, thin from cancer. Big Mac smiled and looked at him and said, "Fuckin' aggravatin' crossing the pond, huh?"

Every Bit
of Twelve

By next afternoon, the *COLUMBIANNA* was halfway down the English channel.

Through the crackle of the VHF came the voice of a man quite alarmed.

"Brixham Coast Guard, Brixham Coast Guard, calling Brixham Coast Guard. This is *Margarita.* Come in."

Tssssshhhhhhhhttt.

"Come in, *Margarita.*"

"I have a warship on my port bow and it's firing on me."

"Say again, *Margarita?*"

"I say he's firing on me. Star shells. They seem to be landing pretty close to me. *Over.*"

"*Weeeeeeooooooooooweeeeeeettt.*"

"Right. Switch to channel sixty-three."

"Sixty-three."

"Do you receive?"

"All clear."

"Right. *I say there's a WARSHIP off my bow and he's FIRING, repeat, FIRING on me and the shells are getting bloody CLOSE. OVER.*"

The Captain, who was standing by the VHF set on the bridge, grinned. "That's real tough shitsky, ain't it?" he said.

Fssssssht . . .

"Warship Ajax, warship Ajax, this is Brixham Coast Guard. Come in, Ajax."

"Right, *Margarita*, the ship that is firing is the H.M.S. *Ajax*. I can't raise him from here. The navy are in the process of trying to raise him."

"Yes, well—"

"I'll have another go. I'll have a go."

"How do *I* get *Ajax*? They're getting closer, you know."

"Warship Ajax, warship Ajax, this is Brixham."

"—still firing star shells at the moment. It looks like—"

"They won't hurt you."

"This water's rough enough as it is."

"They won't hurt, *Margarita*."

Tsssssssshhhhhht.

Just after dark three hours later, the *Columbianna* nosed in to Torbay to drop Captain Swindells. The Captain invited him to his cabin for a farewell drink. Captain Swindells told him he had started as a bank clerk years ago in Yorkshire, advancing to assistant manager. One day the manager told him he had no future at the bank. He explained that he was in all respects an exemplary worker, but that if he were in line for the top job years ahead, the board of directors would immediately eliminate him from the list of candidates on the grounds that no man named Swindells should be president of a bank.

"You're joking," said Swindells.

"I'm not," said the manager.

So he left the bank and went to a shipping line. After giving him a job, the president of the line handed him a whiskey and told him, "You've come to the right place." Swindells asked why that was so.

"Well," said the president, "we've already got a Captain Cheatham and a Captain Robb."

When the pilot boat drew alongside, Captain Swindells climbed down the Jacob's ladder. He hesitated at the bottom to time the waves that were agitating the pilot boat, then leaped onto the deck, where two men grabbed him to safety. A light line was thrown, and a man on the pilot boat tied a wet roll of

172

newspapers to it. Cascabel hauled it aboard. Before disappearing below, Swindells waved good-bye at the *Columbianna*'s bridge. The pilot boat gunned its engine and sped off to Torbay, where warm cups of tea, family, and a hot fire were waiting.

A short article in the *Times* of London commemorated the events of forty years ago to the day as it happened—December 13, 1939—when His Majesty's light cruisers *Ajax* and *Achilles* engaged the pocket battleship *Admiral Graf Spee* and chased her into Montevideo harbor, where the captain scuttled her five days later, tricked into thinking the entire Royal Navy was on its way. *Ajax's* modern-day namesake was apparently concentrating its fire on less formidable prey.

Also in the packet was the *International Herald Tribune.* On page two a photograph, captioned INTRUDER IN THE DUST, depicted one of the captured Russian T-62 tanks the *Columbianna* had brought over from Israel. Now it was in Wiltshire on British army maneuvers, rumbling out of a hedgerow in a whirlwind of twigs.

The morning after Captain Swindells disembarked at Torbay, the barometer dropped 12 millibars in an hour and a half. That's rare. The Captain had only once before seen a barometer do that. This time, it went on falling, bottoming out at 29.24 inches. By nine o'clock that night the seas were up to forty feet. Gusts came out of the southwest at seventy knots, better than eighty miles per hour, gusting to ninety and higher. The Captain cut her engines to half speed, and hove to by putting her nose into the wind.

Just before midnight the Captain said the storm was Force Ten, but by 5:00 A.M., having been thrown against a few bulkheads, he said it was "every bit of Twelve."

Ten and Twelve are indicators on the Beaufort scale. The Beaufort scale was devised in 1805 by Comdr. Francis Beaufort, later Admiral and Knight Commander of the Bath, as a way of measuring the force of wind at sea. Originally it gauged the effect of the wind on a fully rigged man-of-war. Captain Fitzroy of the H.M.S. *Beagle,* which took Darwin to the Galapagos, was among the first generation of navigators to use it. It became official in

1874, when it was adopted by the International Meteorological Committee.

The scale runs from 0 ("calm—sea like a mirror") to 12 ("hurricane—the air is filled with foam and spray; sea is completely filled with driving spray; visibility very seriously affected"). After a monstrous storm in 1955, the U.S. Weather Bureau added some additional numbers—13 to 17. One navy booklet notes, below a photo of a pretty horrible looking Force Twelve storm, that "Photographs of conditions above thirteen are not available."

The storm that hit the *Columbianna* was the second worst the Captain had seen in thirty-six years of sailing. The roughest had been Typhoon Dinah. Dinah struck the Philippine Sea in October 1967 while Captain Lee was on the *American Victory* with a cargo of telephone poles and Kotex. Her winds were clocked at 140 knots, over 160 mph. The official weather advisory described the seas as "mountainous and phenomenal." All the paint was rubbed off the *Victory*'s stern by sea spray. The Captain didn't leave the bridge for three days.

Though he had been through that and other bad storms, this gale worried him a bit. The sea was almost completely white, and the force of the wind made it hard to stay hove to. It kept pushing her bow away from the direction of the oncoming gusts and into danger. The most perilous thing that can happen to a ship in such seas is to be broached: taken broadside by a bad wave. It often results in capsizing.

The waves were not visible until they were right on top of her, and the faint glow cast on them by the mast lights seemed to accentuate their enormity. They scared Butts so much that he said he couldn't stand being sober. The wind blew his beard flat against his face as he clung to the wing deck rail looking out into the loud darkness.

As waves collapsed out from under her, the *Columbianna*'s bow slammed down into the troughs, burying her foredeck in water. One wave covered everything forward of midships. She heaved up out of the watery tonnage with an imperturbable grace, like an old mother bear shaking off an avalanche. Mr. Dexter spoke to her encouragingly, "Come on, *come on.*" Another wave struck before her decks had emptied of the previous one. "Stop that," he said. By the end of his four-hour watch he was exhausted. The storm had tried his patience. As he left the bridge, he said, to no one in particular, "This is fucking *ridiculous.*"

A broadside from a rogue wave gave the entire crew an intimation of mortality. Rogue waves are higher than and travel contrary to the prevailing sea. No one saw this one coming. It hit with an unnerving *ka-boom,* and pushed the 21,700-ton ship forty degrees over on her side. Two-hundred-and-thirty-pound Bob Cascabel was on the port wing deck, suddenly found himself staring into close and chaotic white water. A stool at the end of the bridge flew fifteen feet in the air, smashed an electrical panel, bounced off a bulkhead, sailed out into the darkness, and ricocheted suicidally off the wing deck railing into the North Atlantic. After she was hit, the ship's superstructure vibrated for eight seconds.

Just then, the door between the chart room and the bridge banged open.

"Gawd-*dammit!*"

Usually Higgin arrived for his watch less dramatically, but he was angry. "Je-sus Chr-*ayst.*"

He wiped his wire-rimmed spectacles. He had been below in his focsle reading *Tai-Pan* when the rogue wave struck.

"Shook me outa my bed, threw me onto the deck," he said. "I go outside to see if we took any damage and my nostrils get flattened by the wind. I even got *welts* on my neck from the collar flappin'."

He shivered in the wet.

"Made me rip a page outa my book." He groped in his slicker pockets. "I got it here somewhere. Page 317. Good page, incidentally. I was just turnin' that page when we hit that son of a bitch" —he produced the orphaned page—"an' it went *rip.*"

Higgin said Big Mac was knocking on doors below, asking for Rolaids. "Mr. Darby told Big Mac to get him a tube a Rolaids cause he'd eaten spaghetti *and* fried oysters for dinner and he was complainin' of an upset stomach. I told Mac to tell him, 'Yeah, if you're lookin' for sympathy you'll find it right there in the dictionary between *shit* and *syphilis.*' "

Next morning, after a sleepless night, there was the usual catastrophe in the pantry. Slim and Gut had not yet mastered the business of Making Ready to Put to Sea, that is, nailing down every loose object. Perhaps because they themselves were not Ready to Put to Sea.

Slim hovered near his friend. Gut's head and shoulders had disappeared into the steel sink. Gut's *ooooo*s echoed in it.

"Man," Slim said to Cascabel, as he tried to coax Gut into swallowing a saltine cracker for the nausea, "you know them phorporus thangs you told me about? That light up? Jellyfish or somethin'? Man, I was watchin' them damn phorporus jellyfish goin' by my window all night long. I told Gut about 'em but he don' even want to look. An' that wave—damn—when I open my eyes to see if I still alive—you know that big chest in my room? —well, it *flew*. I said to Gut, 'Gut, you see that? We got to tie that thang down.' He say, 'No, Slim. Ain' make no sense movin'.' "

Gut shook and shuddered. Poor Gut, poor seasick Gut. The Ghost, untroubled by the storm and apparently trying to make Gut feel better, talked in his singsong Norwegian way about how much vorse it vas vay back den. The Ghost was a kind and Christian man, though a bit crazy.

"By de time ve reach Maine," he said of his first transatlantic passage, "it look like our ship vas coming in from de North Pole, from de Ardic. *Aye-cicle all over.* And ve riding trou dat storm, in de North Atlantic, two o'clock at night, me and my rooom-mate.

"Uch," said Gut.

"Two o'clock at night—dat sea, you know, is de most power-ful ting in God's creation. Dere is naw-ting more, more powerful dan dat, and break steel like a *matchstick.* And break de porthole, ja. Two o'clock, here ve are svimming in our bunks, vader up to here. And ve are svimming amongst millions and millions and millions of cockroaches. Big *and* small. Dis before de days ven dey fumigating."

176

"Urgg—"

"Dey have so many of dem in dose days. I used to see dem in de messhall having de rice cereal. Big fat one in my tea once—"

"Hey, man," said Slim, "don't be talkin 'bout no cockroaches."

"Oh! dat storm! God really lead us trou dat storm, dat's for sure. His strong hands behind de vheel. Vatching over us all de time. No doubt about *dat!* Ve vere all small men. Felt kind of small and helpless. Dere's no ocean like de Atlantic. No—and she —ven de Atlantic get mad—ay yi *yi!*"

Mr. Fogarty, the Chief Mate, was delighted by the storm, since it preoccupied the Captain. As soon as the Captain left the messhall, he began to talk about another storm he had been through with him. "You never seen a man so terrified. Two crossings ago we lost a train car, a locomotive, due to sheer misjudgment. Severe storm. He went off course to accommodate it, then decided arbitrarily to go back on course. He said, 'We're wasting too much time.' I said, 'Well, why not? Longer it takes the ship to get in, the more money it makes. As long as you got weather they can't complain.' But he took a sharp turn back onto course, she pitched over fifty degrees, and the locomotive went right over the side." He chuckled at the memory and walked off.

By noon she was near the spot where the mine had been sighted. By now the French navy would have removed it. Still, some crewmen had a mental image of it rolling murderously down the sides of a big wave, the Captain trying to shoot it with his .38.

Progress was slow against the storm. The engines were still at half ahead, but her speed averaged only 0.23 knots, or 5.7 miles per day, against 384 miles on a normal day.

Usually, if the ship's speed dropped below 16 knots, she went off-hire. The charterer, that is, the company that had hired the ship for this specific voyage, paid a basic daily rate of $10,055, as well as approximately $8,300 a day in fuel costs. But unless a speed of sixteen knots—"sea speed," it's called—is maintained, the charterer doesn't have to pay the $10,055 rate. So every hour the ship is off-hire costs the *Columbianna*'s owners $419. Unless, that

177

is, the weather conditions are Force Five or above. Force Five means winds up to twenty-one knots and eight-foot waves—enough to prevent a ship from maintaining sea speed. When such conditions prevail, the ship is exempted from the off-hire provision and the charterer has to pay, even though her speed is less than sixteen. There was something odd about the *Columbianna's* log books: she never seemed to sail in *any* conditions under Force Five. The words "calm" or "light" hardly occurred at all. The Captain admitted with a wink of the eye that wherever the *Columbianna* went it was always Force Five or better.

During the day the gale eased slightly, and the Captain adjusted her course so that she was no longer headed into the wind. The waves were causing her to roll, about twenty-five degrees, which is safe—over forty gets dangerous. Her period of roll was consistent. Each ship's period of roll is different. The *Columbianna's* was between thirteen and sixteen seconds. If she took longer, it meant her weight was too high. When there was a lot of cargo on deck, she often had this problem. If the roll took less than thirteen seconds—a "snap roll"—it meant the weight in the holds was too low. So far, her period of roll was within the limits.

Something else was worrying the Captain, however, and it had to do with the unusually pervasive smell of Bunker C fuel.

The Captain rang the engine room and Chiefy came to the phone. Yeah, Chiefy said, he'd meant to explain it earlier: one of his oilers had accidentally spilled a little bit of Bunker C into the number three cargo hold.

"How much?" asked the Captain.

"Oh," said Chiefy, "nothin' we can't clean up."

"How much oil?"

"Ah, 'bout—no more'n about fifteen tons."

"Fifteen tons?"

"Well, yeah."

"Fifteen *tons?"*

"No more'n that."

"Jesus *Christ,* Chief."

The Captain hung up silently. He tried to find words.

The handle of the ship's whistle vibrated, and the noise was aggravating the Captain's already worn nerves. "See if you can shut that damn thing up, will you?" he said.

Cascabel looked about for some makeshift wadding. He finally took the Iranian ensign—the little Iranian flag flown when in that nation's waters—out of the signal rack and jammed it between the handle and the bulkhead. It worked.

"Okay, Captain?"

"Can't think of anythin' better to do with it."

Half an hour later the Captain was again on the phone to Chiefy. "Whaddya done about that oil, Chief?"

"I'll get to it, Captain. Don't worry."

"Look here, Chief, you gotta lot of oil floatin' around down there in the number three, right? Now all you gotta do is press a button, right? Hopefully. All right." He hung up.

A few hours later Mr. Dexter heard a loud alien *screeking* noise coming from the middle king post. He called the Captain, who appeared wearing the white jumpsuit, face scarred with pillow-creases. Mr. Fogarty came up, the Bosun came up. They all looked through the bridge windows—to where the now unpinned one hundred twenty-ton-capacity boom swang back and forth. The greater the roll, the louder the *screek*. A winch brake had worked loose, so the boom was no longer tightly cradled in its upright position. Finding out just how loose it was would have required going forward across open deck to the control house. Since every seventh wave or so put the decks underwater, such a course of action would have been foolhardy. So they did the only thing they could—worried about it out loud.

"I don't like it," said the Captain.

"Me neither," said the Bosun.

"I'm already hove to," said the Captain. "I can't bring her up any further."

"I reckon it'll hold."

"What about the gooseneck. You reckon that'll hold?"

"No tellin'."

"What do you think, Chief?" the Captain asked Mr. Fogarty.

"That boom weighs forty-five tons," he answered.

179

"I *know* that."

On the discussion went, accompanied by the *screeking*. The brake on the topping lift winch held through the night.

By nine the next morning the seas had subsided sufficiently to allow the Bosun and the Chief Mate to go forward and secure the boom. They decided to go up to the bow as well and check the cement over the chain pipe. During an ocean passage, the top of the hawsepipe, through which the anchor chain runs, is cemented over to keep incoming seas from filling the chain locker with corrosive salt water. But the sea had smashed through, and the cement was all gone. They'd have to pump out the chain locker.

Then suddenly the bow was under three feet of water.

The water slammed the Bosun beneath the anchor winch. The Chief Mate was hurled thirty feet, and would have gone over except for the life rail. As the sea jetted clear of the foredeck, the Bosun scrambled to his feet and gagged up a pint of seawater. He looked for Mr. Fogarty. Up on the bridge, Mr. Dexter had seen it happen. His hand was on the whistle, ready to blow Man Overboard. The Bosun ran aft, shouting "Chief! Chief!" When he saw him, Mr. Fogarty was unconscious, his head hanging limp over the side of the gunwale. The Bosun shook him awake.

"Chief, you okay?"

"I can't . . . breathe," said Mr. Fogarty. "I think my leg is broken."

Blood was seeping through his khakis. Pooch and Cascabel ran forward, carried him to his focsle. The wound was a deep four-inch gash along the shin. He took breaths in gulps. But he refused first aid and asked to be left alone in his cabin.

An hour later the auto alarm in Sparks's cabin went off. He put on the headphones and listened:

CQD . . .
VESSEL 18,000 TON M/T BONOMO GASOIL HEAVY
WEATHER VERY ROUGH DAMAGE TO DECK PLATE IN
MIDDLE SHIP

NUMBER SIX CARGO TANK AND SIDE STOP PSN AT 0655
GMT 45'
05N 07' 50W 105 MILES N OF LA CORUNA STOP 37
CREW IMMEDIATELY NEED HELP IN CASE ABANDON-
ING. . . .

Sparks radioed station EAR in Spain, which had relayed the message, and gave them the *Columbianna*'s position. CQD is a radio prefix meaning emergency. If CQD is used, the airwaves must be kept clear. The code itself is nicknamed "Come Quick, Distress."

The *Bonomo* was more than a hundred miles away. Sparks listened as Norwegian, Danish, Indonesian, and British ships, all closer, reported in. EAR relayed another CQD:

FRENCH TRAWLER MONTCENIS URGENT FROM LAND'S
END SEVEN MEN ABOARD STOP FISHING NET CAUGHT IN
SCREW. . . .

An hour later, another message came in from the *Bonomo:*

COURSE 110 SPEED 10 STOP NOTHING CHANGE ON MY
TANKS I DISCHARGE SOME CARGO TO SEA.

"What I don't get," said Sparks, lighting a new cigarette off the butt of the last, "is how come he's doing ten knots if he's sinking? Sounds screwy to me."

Sparks's skepticism was not out of line with the realities. Of the five hundred merchant ships that went down in 1979, Lloyd's of London estimates that over one hundred of them were sunk on purpose. Sparks said that after a storm was a good time to sink a ship, that it always looked better that way.

The practice of sinking ships for insurance has in fact become so commonplace, particularly on Panamanian, Liberian, and Greek ships, that there are stories about notorious captains famed for their expertise in sending ships to the bottom. One such captain, a Greek, is so well-known—and feared—by Greek crews that when he boards a new ship, the crew waits by the

181

gangway to see how much luggage he's brought. If he arrives with a suspiciously small bag, the men start making signs of the cross, and many jump ship.

A Dutchman asked the *Bonomo* for a bearing. Her radio operator held down the wireless key for ten seconds, sending a continuous signal the Dutchman and other ships could home in on.

Forty-five minutes later there was a sudden burst of transmissions:

NORWEGIAN VESPAYAN IN DISTRESS AREA

DANISH VESSEL CHARLOTTE HAS 10 CREW MEMBERS ON BOARD

INDONESIAN HILAR 12 ON BOARD

GERMAN TUG CARIBIC IN DISTRESS POSITION

Finally there was one last message from the *Bonomo:*

NOW ABANDONING SHIP AND TRANSFERRING VESPAYAN

"At least he stayed with his ship to the end."

"Sure he stayed with his ship to the end," said Sparks. "He had to make sure she went down."

The last transmission Sparks picked up that busy morning was about two empty lifeboats found off Land's End. By late afternoon, the gale's death toll had risen to forty. The English coastline reportedly took severe damage, and would show it for months. At sea all that remained were abandoned life rafts and oil slicks. "The sea is feline," wrote Oliver Wendell Holmes. "It licks your feet—its huge flanks purr very pleasant for you; but it will crack your bones and eat you, for all that, and wipe the crimsoned foam from its jaws as if nothing had happened."

Four hours after the wave struck him, Mr. Fogarty was sitting at his desk working on the crew's overtime sheets, and by suppertime even his limp was gone. His recovery was remarkable, especially for a man of almost seventy. It was then Mr. Fogarty made an admission that explained a great deal—he was a Christian Scientist. No wonder he wasn't interested in thermometers. He said not to share the secret with anyone, correctly assuming that the men would not be reassured to know their chief medical officer had never in his life opened a medical book.

_____*Snug Harbor*

SEAFARING IS A ROUGH LIFE THAT AGES A MAN QUICKLY. THOUGH immeasureably improved since the old days, the illness and injury rate is still remarkable. Since the mid-1950s, it has ranged from a high of ninety-one percent to a low of sixty-five percent among deep sea merchant seamen. By the end of the seventies, seven out of ten seamen became sick or were hurt on the job. The total V.D. rate, however, is less than one percent.

Different kinds of ships contribute to different ailments. Tanker crews have a high rate of respiratory infection. Containership crews, who travel rapidly and frequently between varying climates, have a high rate of endocrine disease, arthritis, and rheumatism. And the crews of tramp freighters have the highest incidence of gum disease and V.D.—possibly because they spend a lot of time in port, having contact with foreign bodies.

Some of the survivors of the rough life have settled at a place called Snug Harbor. Many of them first went to sea during the last days of the sailing vessels. For them it has been a long trip.

The road to Sea Level, North Carolina—Highway 70—runs straight east out of Beaufort along the outer banks, past pesticide and Baptist billboard ads shot up by bullets from .22s. Twenty miles beyond Moorehead City, the road twists. There are sharp turns, some of them well-known. In 1979, a carload of drunk young marines from the nearby base rounded a curve and crashed;

185

they were all killed. Cedar Island, just north of Sea Level, may be the site of the Lost Colony, where English settlers came ashore but died during a hard winter because the relief ship couldn't find the same inlet again. Kitty Hawk is not far. Nearby Nag's Head is named for pirates who used to mount lanterns on horseback and ride the beaches. Mariners took the lanterns for navigation lights and drove their ships up on the shoals. Cape Hatteras is also not far, site of so many wrecks that ships have sunk, decades apart, on top of each other. The outer banks are heavily fished and crabbed, and lately they have become off-loading spots for South American marijuana. Hundreds of marshy inlets offer good cover. The Coast Guard is wise to it, and state police watch Highway 70 for vans with out-of-state license plates. Local people are upset about skyrocketing drug use in the county. At night possums and cottonmouths cross the highway on the double. Some instinctive natural selection may tell them that gassed marines and drug smugglers do not brake for them.

Four years ago, an old man hummed down Highway 70 in an electric wheelchair, driving toward the only intersection in Sea Level. Not far behind him, and closing the gap, was a young woman who'd had a pretty hard day already without having to chase old sailors down the interstate. She caught up with him.

"Leo," she said, out of breath. "What the *hell* are you doing here?"

"Going to town to get me a drink."

"You can't drive that thing out here."

"Why not?"

"Because—because you don't have a *license,* that's why." Sandra Venegoni is a captain in the Army Reserves, which may be where she learned calm under fire. She wheeled Leo back to the grounds; later, battery acid spilled on her stockings. It was that kind of day. In the morning, she and the staff of the Sailors' Snug Harbor had moved over a hundred old seamen from the Harbor's former location on Staten Island, New York, to its new one in Sea Level.

The idea for Sailor's Snug Harbor was born when Capt. Robert Richard Randall, Jr., son of a notorious but eventually

186

respectable privateer of the revolutionary war era, made out his will on June 1, 1801. His father had left him a whopping estate. Randall junior provided for his children, disposed of his gold sleeve buttons, specified a sum of money for the "legitimate children" of his brother, and then, in death-shaky hand, signed over "the rents fines and profits of the said rest residue and remainder of my said real and personal Estate, to erect and build upon some eligible part of the land upon which I now reside an Asylum or Marine Hospital to be called 'The Sailors' Snug Harbor' for the purpose of maintaining and supporting aged decrepid and worn out sailors." Aside from various houses on Liberty, Stone, Water, and other streets in New York City, and a plantation on the Pee Dee River in South Carolina, the bulk of Randall's land was then a farm. That land now covers a hugely valuable rectangle of New York City real estate north of Washington Square, bounded on one side by Fifth Avenue from Seventh to Tenth streets and running across town to the Bowery. One Fifth Avenue, a well-known apartment house, was built on this property in 1929, causing a journalist of the period to write that Snug Harbor had "the best paying farm in America." New York University now holds a long-term lease on the entire parcel. Its value, conservatively estimated, is about $25 million. At the time of the bequest, the land was two miles north of the city limits.

Randall's will was of course contested. The legend is that Randall asked his old friend Alexander Hamilton for advice on what to do with his money, and Hamilton said he should return it to the sailors, without whom his father could not have taken such prizes on the high seas. There is no evidence that this conversation took place. Still, a large oil of Hamilton hangs prominently in the Harbor dining hall. Randall may have determined to endow an old sailors' home because in 1801 the United States had yet to build a marine hospital. At any rate, after his death, quite a few people felt left out. They hired lawyers, and began the legal battles. The last to contest the will was the Episcopal bishop of Nova Scotia, who claimed he was Randall's descendant on the distaff side. His lawyer, Daniel Webster, argued the case on up to the U.S. Supreme Court, but lost. The will was not resolved until 1830. Meanwhile, Manhattan had become so developed that the trustees, rather than build Snug Harbor on the property and lose the valuable rents, bought land across from the island.

The Harbor was constructed on a beautiful, sprawling, 130-acre tract of land on the north shore of Staten Island overlooking the Kill van Kull. The architecture was Greek revival. There were dormitories, a library, infirmary, chapel, morgue, and a splendid old memorial church—since torn down—that was a scale replica of Saint Paul's cathedral in London. Sweeping lawns, statuary, and fountains completed the grounds. The chief administrator of the Harbor was called "governor"—the traditional English title given to heads of institutions. The Sailors' Snug Harbor opened August 1, 1833. Among its original residents were: Peter Nelson, New York, age fifty-five, crippled by rheumatism; William Collins, Prussia, age sixty, same complaint; George Thompson, Connecticut, twenty-nine, weak knees; James Webster, England, forty-five, frost-bitten; George Whitley, Louisiana, twenty-three, blind.

Another reason the trustees chose Staten Island as a site was their fear that Manhattan would expose the residents "to many temptations . . . considering the habits and character of seamen." Sure enough, by 1836 the trustees' minutes were full of baleful incidents involving demon rum: "There have been several instances of individuals having been found beastly drunk upon the road and brought home by strangers to the disgrace of the Institution and mortification of the sober part of its members." The iron fence that still surrounds the land was put up not long afterward, not so much to keep people out, as in. The men were given a daily ration of cider, which they were able to trade to locals for hard liquor.

Randall made no mention of religion in his will, but those were revivalist times, and with a rector and senior minister on the board of trustees, the Harbor concluded that it was not enough to nourish the sailors' bodies. Their souls as well were certainly in need of feeding. "You are here," Reverend Phillips admonished the old salts in a guest lecture on Sunday, not to spend your time in idleness, in the mere animal indulgence of eating, and drinking, and sleeping; but you are here to *refit.* Your voyage has not yet terminated; the most important part of it is yet before you; there are quicksands, concealed rocks, whirlpools and yawning gulphs. There may be a darker, severer, and more terrific storm, and a more awful waving of the elements still in reserve for you, than any through which you have ever passed—you may yet be hopelessly wrecked, and left to sink into the deep and unfathomable abyss. Have you prepared your bark for this last part of your voyage, and are you sure all is right? Are you making daily observations, watching the clouds and the winds, and the tides, and are you habitually ready to launch at any moment? Above all, have you engaged Him who alone can pilot you safely through this dangerous sea into the haven of eternal rest?

Hopeless wrecks, whirlpools and yawning gulphs. Are you ready to *launch?* The preachers, Women's Christian Temperance Union ladies, and others who have auctioned off salvation to generations of sailors in bethels and floating churches and skid-row missions have truly meant well, but faced with a congregation of reprobate seadogs they have never been able to resist calling God a pilot. On some occasions He is promoted to Admiral of the Fleet.

Reverend Phillips waxed rather mean-spirited in the bit about the "mere animal indulgence of eating, and drinking, and sleeping." Father Mapple, who preached to Ishmael and Queequeg at the start of *Moby Dick,* took a better tack: "Woe to him who seeks to pour oil upon the waters when God has brewed them into a gale! . . . Woe to him whose good name is more to him than goodness! . . . Woe to him who would not be true, even though to be false were salvation! Yea, woe to him who, as the great Pilot Paul has it, while preaching to others is himself a castaway!"

Thomas Melville, Herman's younger brother, was governor from 1867 to 1884. By all accounts he was an embezzler and a martinet. He was at any rate very unpopular. Among his reforms

189

—work requirements, "tabooing" whereby a seaman's tobacco could be taken away—was a new set of bylaws requiring residents to sign a temperance pledge and to attend chapel "at least once every Sunday." Nonetheless, Theodore Dreiser visited in 1904 and found "when Sunday comes, not one out of ten attends religious services." One old fellow told him, "I haint had much time for preachin' for sixty-eight years . . . and I 'spec' I'll manage to weather it out and get to port without worryin' much about it—the little time I have left. I ain't disrespectful, you understand —just kind of set."

All of the original Harbor's residents eventually made the trip to Monkey Hill, the cemetery hidden by a pond at the end of a long, tree-shaded avenue. (In the days when sailors had masts to climb, they were sometimes called "monkeys.") It is a steep hill. In winter, graves were dug early, before the ground froze. There were always enough men to fill the holes before spring. Today the cemetery is hard to find, and is tended by a nearby orphanage. Its gate is locked and all but a few of the gravestones have been removed to discourage vandals. Kids do manage to sneak over the fence, though, and impale Budweiser cans on its spikes.

During the mid-1970s the City of New York fought a lengthy and bitter legal battle against the Harbor's trustees to prevent it from moving. They didn't want to lose a living landmark. But new fire codes had made it virtually impossible to maintain the old Harbor, and some of its structures had badly deteriorated. The trustees won the suit, found a sweetheart deal on land in Sea Level, and in 1976 they made the move.

Some men at the new Harbor in Sea Level remember the sinking of the *Maine*. Some were shipwrecked in the days when all a crew could do was run up a distress flag and hope. One man is a member of the four hundred surviving "Old Contemptibles," the original one hundred fifty thousand British foot soldiers who fought in the trenches during World War I. One made trips up the Congo River when it was a heart of darkness. Another lost an uncle in the battle of Vicksburg. Quite a few have over fifty years of sea time. One sailed on the same ship for thirty-one years. The day Captain Bowley arrived in Sea Level, both legs amputated above the knee, he sat in the office for a bit, looking out the window at the pine trees and flagstaff, and said, "This is the last ship, and it ain't goin' nowhere."

The hundred-odd residents live in a $6 million brick building on the edge of a marsh. It's a labyrinthine single story, nothing gloomy about it. Sunshine floods through glass walls and skylights. Old oils of clipper ships and barks decorate the walls. The dining room is festooned with the Snug Harbor collection of ensigns and union jacks. Everyone has his own room, phone, television, radio. There are lounges, a workshop, therapy rooms, a snack bar called the "Bumboat" that serves a good cheeseburger, a library, theater, a chapel with stained glass windows from the memorial church, ship models—plenty of the old to dignify the new. The infirmary wing has forty beds, all private and well equipped. The Sea Level hospital is a hundred yards down the highway. But most residents die at the Harbor, surrounded by everything they need, even the pilotage, if they want it, of Monsignor Mullin, an eighty-year-old retired navy chaplain who has been listening to sailors' confessions for half a century and who is not easily scandalized on the Lord's behalf.

The only requirement for admission to the Harbor—aside from having reached the end of the tether—is ten years of merchant sailing, five of them under the U.S. flag. Applicants have to fill out financial statements, but the total cost of board, food, and complete medical care is—nothing. Residents are allowed to contribute if they wish, but no more than $70.00 a month. That comes out to $2.30 per day; not unreasonable for one of the best-run old folks homes in America.

The waiting list to get into the Harbor is long, but in urgent cases the trustees make room. There are no rules, no requirements for church attendance, and residents can come and go as they please, take vacations, trips, whatever. Cocktails are served every day in the infirmary to those who want them. Residents can buy their own liquor on excursions into Beaufort or have the staff buy it for them. Wild drunkenness is not encouraged. Fighting is grounds for dismissal, but at that age most of the fight has gone out of a man. Discipline is not totally lacking. This notice was up by the cash register at the Bumboat:

> Captain Jack Coldin *may* buy cigarettes from the Bumboat but *may not* buy matches.
>
> —The Governor

No matter what rating they held on retirement, everyone at the Harbor is called "Captain." It's a traditional courtesy borne of pragmatism: no one can pull rank. Some residents call themselves "Snuggies."

Seamen have a reputation for outlandish storytelling, largely well deserved—a prerogative of the lonely. A hundred ancient mariners under one roof could tell a whole lot of stories, except everyone has heard them already. Sailors are wary consumers of each others' anecdotal goods. Dreiser recorded of one bit of dialogue:

> "I hain't a-goin' to hear sich rubbish," remarked one seaman, who had taken offence at another's detailed account of his terrible experience in some sea fight of the Civil War. "Sich things ain't a-happenin' to common seamen."
>
> "Yuh don't need to, yuh know," sarcastically replied the other. "This here's a free country, I guess, 'cept for criminals, —and they hain't all locked up, as they should be."
>
> "So I thought when I first seed yuh."

Much is expected of a sea story: wicked storms and women, North Atlantic torpedoings, infernal sea captains, shark-encircled life rafts. The students from Williams College who used to troop out to Arrowhead, Melville's farm near Pittsfield, Massachusetts, didn't go so much to talk "ontological heroics" with the author of *Typee, Omoo, Redburn,* and *White-Jacket,* but to see the man who'd lived with cannibals. ("Think of it!" he complained to Hawthorne. "To go down to posterity is bad enough, anyway; but to go down as a 'man who lived among the cannibals!' ")

192

Almost everyone at the Harbor enjoys a measure of fame owing to some one great episode in the past. The people with five, six, seven, or eight great episodes you wonder about. Those with a single claim to distinction are introduced as such:

"And this is Captain Cronin. He was Captain of the first ship sunk in World War II. Isn't that right, Captain?"

"What's that?"

[Louder] "I say your ship was the first one sunk in World War II."

"That's right."

"I'm sure our visitor would like to hear about it."

"What?"

[Shouting] "I'm sure our visitor would like to hear about it."

"Oh."

Captain Cronin has probably been through that routine one thousand times.

Captain McBride sped around the corner, pushing his wheelchair like a shopping cart. He's not quite resigned to sitting in it. He was seventeen when the *Maine* blew up in Havana harbor. He has owl eyes, wears thick glasses, and a green plastic visor. He pushes the wheelchair at about five miles an hour.

"There goes Captain McBride. HELLO, CAPTAIN!"

"Hello! Hello!"

"You're ninety-nine, aren't you, Captain?"

"Ninety-nine, that's right."

"Didn't you just have your birthday?"

"Got a birthday card from the president."

It was on the seat of his wheelchair, but before there was time to admire it, Peter Campbell was sighted.

Peter was a big Scot, in his seventies. He had emphysema, chain-smoked, was an alcoholic, and was more or less deaf. Still he loved to talk in an incomprehensible brogue, and had a knack for holding people prisoner, unspellbound for hours, while he replayed the cinema of his life, beginning with his first trip to sea at age twelve. Clever mariners steered clear. He slept all day, which left him bright and fresh and itching for a good long talk just when everyone else was exhausted and ready for bed. Craftily, he picked a different spot every night from which to ambush. (Visitors were sometimes asked to make nighttime reconnaissance patrols on behalf of their hosts and to report back on Peter's position. One night he picked his spot so strategically there was simply no way around him. In that case visitors were asked to engage him in conversation so as to create a diversion. Having enjoyed great hospitality, one could not refuse, but went to the duty with a heavy heart.) Peter would admonish those he took into his confidence not to eat the Harbor's bread. "Got *ticks* in't."

Over coffee in the Bumboat one fellow critiqued the carnal pleasures of Valparaiso and Cartagena, preferring the latter for its abundance of thirteen-year-olds. Capt. Arthur Urdahl squirmed. "I can't stand him," he whispered. "He's always talking about his sex life. Screwing this, screwing that. I don't care for that."

Captain Urdahl went to sea at the age of six, around 1908, he thought, aboard a Norwegian barkentine hauling ice and split lumber for aeroplane propellers, from Sweden to England. Eventually he came to America, settled by the Great Lakes, and raised three sons, one of whom was torpedoed in convoy during World War II and killed. He stayed on the same ship from 1928 to 1959 —during which it went through three name changes. He was once caught in a gale on Lake Michigan. By the time it blew over, forty thousand rivets had popped loose. He broke his leg. Then he lost his wife. "I had a stroke," he said, "I ramble a lot."

Eddie Sawyer is usually introduced as the man who was blown into the smokestack when his ship was torpedoed off the coast of South America in 1942. He rolled up his left sleeve to show an ugly scar the length of his arm.

"I was sleepin' on deck right over where it hit," he said, "And when I come down, oh Jesus, I'm in the boilers. Went right into the fuckin' smokestack—'scuse my language." He promised to find the clipping from the New York *World-Telegram*, because he knew it was hard to believe a man could survive falling down a smokestack. But the old clipping would prove it. A few days later

194

Eddie found it, sure enough, and sat his visitor down to read it. It was headlined:

HEROES IN DUNGAREES:
SAILOR 'BURNS IN HELL,'
LIVES TO TELL STORY

It showed a picture of Eddie as a young man. A cigarette hung from his lips. As the ship was "bumped," the story read,

> I went up and up. It seemed like I must have gone up as high as the ship's aerial. Then I started to come down. I was half unconscious, but I realized I was headed right for the stack. I thought I went down the stack, but I must have bounced off it. Everything was all soot, and I was burnin' up all over. I felt like I was cookin' up. I thought I was actually burnin' up in the fires of hell.

"It's a good thing you didn't fall down the smokestack, Eddie."

"Whaddya mean?"

He reread the clipping and scratched the back of his neck.

"They musta got it wrong," he said, sounding disappointed. "I definitely went down that fuckin' smokestack—pardon the language."

Lars Janson was a live-wire Swede, who, if his stories were true, had had an eventful life. Lars stood six feet two and was built like a boxer. He was almost seventy, yet his hair was still blond and crew-cut. He built boats in the workshop and kept a few Heinekens in his fridge. He calculated that his savings account would be exhausted in 1986—"but vhy save money for vhen you can't do anytink vit?"

Lars will most likely not go gently into that good night. He knocked two U.S. Public Health Service doctors unconscious, one during an argument over whether to amputate his

195

gangrenous leg; the second when a spinal tap made him throw up.

Schoolchildren occasionally visit the Harbor, and he has a little game he plays with them. He tells them he knows exactly where he was when they were born. They give him their birthdays, Lars shuffles through a two-inch stack of discharge papers he keeps in his desk drawer, matches the data, and tells them he was on the S.S. *Oladunk* between Port Said and Malta, or wherever.

He made several runs to Murmansk. On one thirteen-ship convoy his was the only ship that returned. Lars ran away from home when he was very young, leaving a cold and dull small town inside the Arctic Circle. Ships took him to the Spanish Civil War. On the dock in Valencia he picked up a shoe with a foot still inside it. "I vas a kid. Ven you are a kid, it's impression, huh?"

Captain Johnson spent his days outside, under the pines, crutches leaning up against his bench. There had been a hurry to get him in: he didn't have much time left. He sat on the bench, toothless, frail, and collapsed inside dryer-rumpled denim, looking for squirrels to feed. He thought there were not enough squirrels in Sea Level. The "gummint," he said, ought to start a "reservation" here for squirrels and chipmunks. He asked if his visitor wanted to see a picture of his "friend"? From an inside pocket he produced a photograph taken not long ago of him cuddling a koala bear in his arms.

Captain Cronin actually *was* skipper of the *City of Rayville*, the first ship to go down in World War II—on November 9, 1940. He had a whole scrapbook of clippings to prove it. En route from Wayalla to Sydney, carrying five thousand tons of lead and iron ore—not a very buoyant cargo—he slammed into a mine. The blast was heard fifteen miles away. Only one man, Mac Bryan, was killed, because he went back for the chief engineer. The other thirty-seven were saved by fishermen. The Captain sent a one-word telegram to his sisters in Staten Island, "SAFE." Forty years later, he explained that "I never did say much." The sisters, his only remaining family, would have been worried. "I was their meal ticket, you know." He went to sea at thirteen to support the family, and was given his first command at twenty-seven when he was first mate on a ship whose captain died of cancer in Calcutta.

In 1938, he'd had a bad experience with a particular cargo. It was on a run from Calcutta to the United States with a shipment for Frank "Bring 'em Back Alive" Buck, purveyor of exotic animals to leading zoos and to Barnum & Bailey. On that trip, the *City of Rayville* carried 1,500 monkeys, 30 boxes of pythons, 2 cages of bears, 12 cages of Indian birds, 4 black panthers, 6 kangaroos, 1 cage of swans, 3 elephants, and 6 missionaries. A python got loose and chased an AB to his cabin. Not a bit discouraged when the door was slammed, the python beat its head against it. A monkey, cornered atop the tallest mast by the quartermaster's mate, committed suicide by leaping into the Atlantic. The local newspaperman reported in his story on the ship's arrival: "The reason Captain Cronin left his ship the moment it touched the pier was not made known. It was said, however, that he had a headache."

Ritchie Ravnich was not introduced as a maker of folklore, but as "our saddest story here." He came from a maritime family, and had been an engineer on New York City harbor tugboats. His father was among the stevedores who loaded the *Lusitania*'s lower holds with an unpublicized cargo of ammunition. In 1961, Ritchie began to notice a stiffness in his legs. Within a few weeks he was unable to move around the engine room without pain, and was declared Not Fit for Duty. Five years later the arthritis had run through his body and made him a quadriplegic. He is fifty-eight now, otherwise in perfect health. "They said I could live another thirty years," he said one night.

He gets about in a special wheelchair he guides with his mouth. He can scratch his perpetually itchy nose up against a hard-bristle paintbrush attached to the controls. "My own design," he says. His wheelchair was formerly owned by a young man in New Bern, North Carolina, who had been paralyzed from the neck down at nineteen when he dove into shallow water, and

197

who died at thirty-five of uremic poisoning. "You think *I* got it bad?" he said. When his bedroom light is turned off at eight each night, after he watches a TV show called "Tic-Tac-Dough," he thinks about what he most loved to do when he was a boy—skate "like a demon" across frozen ponds in winter. He goes to mass each Sunday morning, and goes to confession at least every two weeks.

He said, "They say God doesn't do anything to you He thinks you can't take,"

Captain Helge, eighty-four, lay dying of emphysema in a room down the hall. He had rickets and a broken shoulder that would not heal before he died. In between gasps for breath he smoked cigarettes and remembered how his ship, a Norwegian brig, left Port Adelaide, Australia, on Christmas, 1927, and hit a terrible storm. The food ran out. Until they crawled into Astoria, Oregon, one-hundred-and-twenty-two days later, the crew subsisted on black coffee and chewing tobacco. Most of the men were too weak to climb rigging or tend sails. One man, a twenty-four-year-old Finn with cancer of the nose, went mad with pain. He pulled all the crew's mattresses and clothes out of their bunks and sea chests, threw them into a pile in his focsle, and crawled underneath it. When they pulled him out, he screamed "dat it vass a *'ship of corpses,'* that ve vere going to put him in de hold on ice vith de 'rest of the corpses.' " The next day the Finn climbed up the rigging, jumped into the Pacific, and died.

Captain Helge spent seventy years at sea. On his withered arms are two tattoos; a blotchy, faded ship and a girl, barely recognizable, that he had had put on in Düsseldorf three days after World War I broke out.

His nurse entered with a tray of hypodermics full of painkillers. Afterward, outside his room, she said he always asked if there was mail. "He once said he hoped he wouldn't get any on the thirteenth," she explained. "Said he was on two ships that went down on the thirteenth, and was superstitious."

The Snuggies who fear death least, according to the director of the infirmary, are the atheists and the believers. Thanaphobia is therefore not very common, since not many in-betweeners reside at the Harbor. Death is not covered up, or euphemized into "expiring" or "passing away," and when a man dies, a hearse comes for his body, not an ambulance, as is the practice at many old age homes. A notice of the death goes up on the bulletin board. One sailor said he liked that, because that way at least *someone* would know he had died, and might remember him. The director, Amie Modigh, has been with many of them at the last hour. Just before he died, a blind sailor said he saw "a ladder and God's hand outstretched and God saying, 'If you can reach my hand, you'll see again.' But he couldn't reach it," she said.

As they near death, some write poems . . . for the first time in their lives, as though to leave more than just their personal effects. Remembrances of war,

> *Pills don't do a damn thing they sent us in*
> *Over the sea's lip the flames hit*
> *our eyes then*
> *the blast rocked us we went in*
> *The tanker crew screamed and fried until she died*
> *nothing we could do except*
> *wonder*
> *if sharks like barbecued people.*

With apologies to Masefield,

> *I must climb up in a tree again*
> *and sit where the seagull warbles;*
> *Where the squirrels run up and down a limb*
> *and the ducks have lost their marbles;*
> *And the squawks and hoots and chirps and squeaks*
> *That all the birds are making*
> *Fill the air around so I can't hear*
> *The dentures down there breaking.*

Good-bye to a friend,

Carlyle de Cost
Father Moore, Catholic service. Graveside Carteret
Memorial Gardens,
Beaufort.
Soft misty rain with an east wind suggesting Maine
coastal weather.
A grey day.
I thought of Carlyle on the Grand Banks fishing
grounds in a
dory, baiting the long lines for cod. The painting by
Winslow
Homer that I like so well and which Carlyle saw in my
house last
summer. The deep clear green color of the Maine
Coast Atlantic
in the summertime.
The ocean is greater than death.

On a still summer night, a woman named Mary padded
along the Harbor's corridors in slippers and a quilted nightgown.
She is one of six women at Snug Harbor. She had run away from
her father's farm in Pennsylvania at the age of fifteen when she
accidentally discovered him planning to marry her off to the son
of a rival farmer. "A big, no good *lug.*" She made it to New York
City and found work with the phone company, but wearied of it
after a few years. Then she stumbled onto a job with United
States Lines, in the nursery of the transatlantic passenger liners.
When rough, stormy seas scared the children in the nursery, she
would read aloud to them from Mother Goose, and soon they
would become quiet and listen and fall asleep, huddled around her
on a make-believe hayloft of pillows and cushions. She spent over
thirty years on those ships, never married, and never returned for
even a short visit to the farm in Pennsylvania.

Mary was on the verge of talking about her life at sea, but
from around a corner twenty yards down the hall came Peter
Campbell, refreshed, wide-awake, and ready to talk, reconnoiter-

ing for listeners. He had spotted them; had plotted his rhumb line and was closing fast. The fires of reminiscence were kindling in his eyes.

Mary saw there was no time for stories.

"Listen," she said, "I been, I done, I seen." Then, having said all that could be said, she went off to her berth on the last ship that was not going anywhere.

Sargasso

"Isn't the sea what Algy calls it: a grey sweet mother? The snotgreen sea. The scrotumtightening sea."

James Joyce
Ulysses

Twelve days out of Bremerhaven the *columbianna* was in the middle of the Sargasso Sea. Life aboard the ship had changed. Whether it was the heat or just a sense of the endlessness and intolerableness of all earthly effort was hard to say, but there it was. People were talking about killing the Bosun.

The Bosun's groin was still hurting him. On top of his taxicab wound, he'd contracted crabs in Bremerhaven. He had his own cure for them—he soaked his groin in kerosene every night. Cascabel wanted to drop a match on him while he was asleep, and see if he caught fire. The Bosun's tantrums and screaming had so aggravated Higgin—peaceful Higgin—that he was saying things like "There's three ways of doin' things: the right way, the wrong way, and the navy way. The navy way is to take an outsized wrench an' go upside the son of a bitch's head an' toss 'im overboard." After listening to a proposal to present the Captain with a petition, one AB said, in a North Carolina drawl, "Hell with all this letter shit. Jus' go inta his focsle, grab 'im by the lapels and say, 'Look, you get the hell offa here for health reasons. *Yer* health, *our* reasons.' "

When he was not yelling and carrying on, the Bosun ran a poker game, at which he lost a lot of money to the Steward and Pooch. He was also making crazy bets: a hundred dollars on the cut of the cards, a hundred on whether pork chops would be served for dinner tomorrow. He had almost no booze left, which put a desperate edge on his drinking. One morning Slim ran up to the Captain's cabin and begged him for just one can of beer. Slim never drank at all, so the Captain asked him why. Slim said the Bosun was going to give him a cuckoo clock in exchange for it. The Captain handed Slim the beer, and shook his head. He was hoping the booze would run out soon. Things were getting out of hand.

Butts was drinking too. One night he got so cockeyed on German corn liquor he passed out in the electrical control room —mistaking it for someone's focsle—and spent the night curled up on the floor next to a bank of circuit breakers and throw-switches. The next day, Butts went directly to his watch on the bridge and steered twenty-degree zigzags, leaving a snaky wake until the Captain relieved him, in a loud sort of way.

The Captain himself had become a bit cranky and fed up. One splendid blue morning he walked onto the bridge. Bob Cascabel, at the helm, greeted him with a jolly "Good morning, Captain."

"G'mornin'," said the Captain. "Lissen, you been throwin' coffee off the bridge?"

"No, sir."

"Well, it's got to stop."

"Yes, sir."

"It always happens during your watch."

Actually, it was Mr. Dexter who was in the habit of throwing coffee grounds. Somehow, they never quite cleared the wing deck, thus causing the smear on the upper decks. But Bob Cascabel was not the kind to inform on his mate.

"There's three places you can be on watch," said the Captain. "One is the wing. One is the bow. And the other," he pointed to the flying bridge, nicknamed "Siberia," "is up there."

"Yes, sir."

Later, the Captain asked Chief Mate Fogarty for a key to his day room. Mr. Fogarty told the Captain what he always told him when he asked for something—that it did not exist—so the Captain furiously told him to cut a key for every single lock on board. There were about two hundred of them.

Mr. Fogarty, his leg weeping pus from the wound he would not treat, didn't rush to the task, there being no hurry for keys not used since 1945. But he was annoyed, and began referring to the Captain, at every opportunity, as "a dangerous man, a dangerous man."

A fire broke out in the engine room when a spark from the Yansons' welding tools flew down a ventilator shaft and landed on a bunch of kerosene-soaked rags heaped in a slick of oil. In seconds the paint locker was ablaze. Engineers grabbed fire extinguishers, but in the excitement forgot to shake them, so all that came out were little emetic spurts. Pandemonium reigned. Chiefy yelled and yelled. The Yansons looked down on the confusion, laughing uncontrollably as the fire was eventually put out and everyone blamed everyone else.

There was fighting. The Baker, unable to endure Yoya's tirades any longer, chased him out of the galley with a knife. Boykin, an AB, accused Jefferson of stealing his laundry bag. Jefferson said an unflattering thing about Boykin's mother. Boykin punched him in the eye. Three people were needed to separate them and in the process Cascabel stepped on Jefferson's balls. Jefferson, suspicious anyway, became convinced there was a conspiracy against him among the whites and took to carrying a crowbar. During meals he slung it over his shoulder. He said that when the ship got in he was going to bring all the "bros" down to the dock and "take care of business."

Big Mac lost patience with his focslemate, Eckert, whom Higgin had lectured about exposing his armpits at dinner. Every night since Charleston Eckert had thrown his used and highly rank underwear on top of Big Mac's toothbrush. Big Mac finally socked him, in the mouth, but picked him up off the deck and apologized for having had to do it.

Bodine and Francis did not overlook many chances to call

each other "nigger" and "you old drunk" when they met in passageways, but this had been going on so long it was clearly a platonic relationship.

Salvador, the Filipino oiler, one of the best-liked, most cheerful men aboard, unaccountably became convinced about this time that someone was planning to pump poison gas into his focsle as he slept. He sealed his door jamb with putty.

The Ghost spent more time on the bow continuing his talks with King Neptune and the "green things." There were so many of them. The pelagic weed was thick enough in parts to resemble, under the light of the new moon, a frosted marsh. Columbus was the first to record the existence of the Sargasso Sea, though it is thought the Carthaginians may have reached it as early as 530 B.C. Most of the world's eels are born here. The elvers swim west, hitchhiking to Europe along the Gulf Stream. For centuries, seamen believed that ships became mired in the thick Sargassum, that their crews died horribly of thirst and hunger, and that the vessels, planks rotted and nibbled away by infauna, eventually sank into the warm, highly saline water of the oceanic eddy. In the middle of all this ocean it was still possible to feel trapped, even pushing along at sixteen knots on a ship built long after the myth.

On Christmas Eve, the *Columbianna* was nearing a passage called Hole-in-the-Wall, south of Great Abaco, Bahamas. From Hole-in-the-Wall she would move into the North East and then the North West Providence Channel, past Stirrup Cay, Great Issac Island, and south into the Straits of Florida. She would hug the curve of the Florida Keys and at the Dry Tortugas, would swing north across the Gulf of Mexico toward New Orleans.

The night was warm. Off to the east, electrical storms lit up the clouds like bombing runs. But the sky over the *Columbianna*'s stack was clear. Stars were visible—Sirius, Betelgeuse, Belatrix. Higgin had the lookout. He walked from the bridge to the wing deck, hands stuffed in his pockets, a lit cigarette in his mouth. He raised his eyes to the lactescent band marking the rim of our galaxy.

"There's thirty thousand *million* o' them rascals up there," he said.

Stars were dropping into the atmosphere with astonishing frequency, one every few minutes. Some left trails covering half the sky. Beneath that great canopy the sea was a mirror. Higgin said she was heading into "the *danger zone:* black women, black rum, and waterspouts."

He talked about Christmases on the family farm in Kentucky. There were stories about drinking toddies "till my wings caught fire," walking the fields in the cold night air and firing shotguns till the barrels turned red. He had not been home for the holidays in fourteen years.

"Fucked up, fed up, and far away from home," he snorted.

Big Mac arrived on the wing deck to relieve Higgin at the lookout. He had beer on his breath, which was surprising since beer was now very scarce. He shook Higgin's hand in his mock formal way, repeating his old bit: "Shake the hand that shook the world." Tonight, his boozy, Irish cheer made him seem old and sad and lonely. Higgin went to his focsle.

Cascabel walked to the main deck, stood under the protruding wing. He smoked a cigarette and watched stars, enormous, glowing, red ones, fall out of the sky. Unusual. He counted five in the space of an hour, wishing on them as they fell.

Young Mr. Darby, the third mate, appeared on deck. The Captain had returned his pistol on the understanding he would discard it before they reached the States. He didn't want to repeat his hassle with German customs—not in the United States. Mr. Darby was holding the gun, trying to decide whether to hide it or throw it overboard. Finally he heaved it into the sea, and watched it sink, a little Saturday Night Special trailing phosphorescent bubbles as far as our eyes could follow.

Cascabel asked Mr. Darby what would cause shooting stars to be red. Mr. Darby said he didn't think shooting stars ever were red. They waited for the next one. After ten minutes, a red light arced off the wing deck. Then they heard a cough, and Cascabel realized he'd been wishing on Big Mac's cigarette butts.

Slim and Gut, and the Yanson brothers, were forward at the bow, where the breeze was strongest. The four of them were counting the hours until the ship docked.

"Hey, Slim," said Gut. "They say we gonna tie up to the Poland Street wharf in N'Ohleans."

"Just as long as we tie up to *somethin'*, Gut."

They liked each other, the Yansons, Slim and Gut. Their deep Southernness, as well as their common hate for the seafaring life, made them allies. They also made each other laugh. But they differed in religious outlook. Slim and Gut had been raised as good Baptist lads, and as long as only a rusty hull separated them from "Mr. Jaws"—as they called whatever was down there, and hungry —there was no point in tempting fate. The Yansons, however, were always making religious jokes—indeed, seemed to tell only jokes with unnervingly blasphemous punch lines.

"We blessed," said Slim, talking about the gale off France. "That storm kill forty people."

"Blessed, hell," said the older Yanson, who grinned and spat a wad of tobacco.

"Don't be startin' that again," said Slim. "Just *don't* be startin' that again."

"Hey," said Yanson, "you know what the drunk told Jesus?"

"No, no, *no,*" said Slim.

"—when he dropped—"

"no—"

"—the Cross?"

"I don't *want* t'know."

" 'You keep droppin' that thing an' they're gonna throw you outa the parade.' "

The Yansons laughed themselves into a ten-year stretch in Purgatory. Slim and Gut, fighting back smiles that went against their better instincts, shook their heads and looked at each other like bystanders at the opening of Pandora's box.

"An' you know, Gut," said Slim, "he gonna live a hunnerd years longer'n us."

"I know, Slim."

"The Lord won' have no place t'put 'im."

"The devil don' wan' him, that's for sure."

"Ain' no place for him."

"Th'ocean. That's th'only place for *that* boy."

_____Gone Shipmates

LAND FELL, AND A HARD LIGHT BLEACHED THE MIAMI SKYLINE.
Mr. Fogarty pointed at the city stretched along the horizon and
said, in the spirit of Christmas Day, "Jewtown."

She stayed close to the Keys to avoid the Gulf Stream's
northerly current. Toward noon the first housefly buzzed aboard.
As she was now within range, Pooch hooked up the TV antenna.
The crew, leaden with mince pies and eggnog, watched afternoon
game shows:

_"Okay now, Teresa, this is for you: What object is most handy
to take care of one of Bob's_ amorous _fits of passion?"_

Off Alligator Reef, she crossed the agonic line, along which
there is no magnetic variation. Squalls had moved up from Cuba.
Warm, aromatic rain sheeted onto her decks. Before midnight
she fetched up the Dry Tortugas light, and turned north toward
the Mississippi River.

At Southwest Pass, the Mississippi was ebbing into the Gulf
of Mexico at two knots. Shoals less than a hundred yards directly
across from the river mouth force a ship to approach at a perpendicular and then swing ninety degrees to the right. When the
current is running this swiftly, the ship must make the turn at sea
speed—sixteen knots—so the river current doesn't have time to
hold her bow off and prevent her from completing the turn. If
she didn't maintain the speed, she would hit the rocks on the
other side of the pass.

The Bosun stood ready at the anchor. Sparks manned his radio transmitter. Big Mac took the helm. The Mississippi river pilot, who had come aboard twenty minutes earlier, peered into the darkness, watching the way the water curled around the end of the breakwater as the ship approached the pass. At what looked like the last possible moment he shouted, *"Hard right."* Big Mac spun the wheel all the way to starboard with one hand. The force of the turn heeled her over to port. The current hit the bow and seemed to hold it, trying to keep the ship from turning, but the river was not strong enough to resist the 78 rpm thrust. The bow swung to the right, aligning with a distant point invisible to all eyes but the pilot's. He quietly ordered, "Midships," and she passed into calm water.

The pilot, Albro Michell, Jr., leaned into the bridge window, and sipped coffee while talking about his life and the river. The two had much in common. His brother and uncle were river pilots; his father had been a river pilot; and so had his grandfather and great-grandfather. He said his great-great-great-great- . . . great- ("I think that's it") grandfather had been the first New Orleans pilot. "Well," he added after a pause, "that's actually on my *wife*'s side." But his son, a mate on a Liberian ship who would soon start pilot training, could claim blood ancestry with the great man who had been the first to read the river and learn its secrets in the 1730s. Michell was pleased to have given his son those ennobling genes. His conversation was peppered with helm commands.

"My other uncle went down on a ship—right five—three miles south of where we came in back there, during World War II. Killed. He was on the *David McKelvy*. Lotta U-boats hung around there. The pilot had just—midships—gotten off. Torpedo passed right under the pilot boat. Steady's she goes."

He was onto the history of Pilottown when a 160-foot oil rig supply boat, about to pass the *Columbianna* on the starboard side, inexplicably cut sharply right across the *Columbianna*'s bow.

"Hard right! Hard right!" yelled the pilot, blowing quick blasts on the ship's whistle. A collision was imminent. Everyone on the bridge braced for the impact. Just then, the other ship's

210

stern slipped under the *Columbianna*'s bow with only feet to spare.

"Midships!" said the pilot. "Five degrees left. *Get his name!*"

The Captain sped to the wing, but the moonlight glare made her name impossible to read.

"He almost bought the farm," said the Captain.

The pilot tried repeatedly to raise the ship on the VHF, but got no response. He called the pilot station at Southwest Passage. "Be *sure* to get his name," he told them, "even if you have to go alongside. We have to report that guy to the Coast Guard." This quickly brought an answer.

"This is the *John Brown,*" said a voice trying hard to sound surprised. "Is someone trying to reach me?"

"This is the *Columbianna.* What happened there? You almost caused a collision."

"Ah, yeah—"

"We were all set for a two-whistle passage and you showed me your red."

"I thought it was a little tight."

"We were right in the middle of the channel—nothin' tight about it. I gave you my horn and you didn't do a thing. Just kept going. What was going on there, anyway?"

Pause.

"I left the wheelhouse there for a moment." Pause. "Guess it was the wrong moment."

"Well, okay, man, but you gotta watch out. This is a big ship here. We could have killed you."

"Yeah. Me and everyone on this ship."

Toward dawn, a few hours down river from New Orleans, a passing tanker spoke the *Columbianna.*

"Zat you, Albro?"

"Yes, sir. That you, John?"

"Yo. Mornin'."

"Morning, John."

"What kinda ship zat, Albro?"

"She's a heavy lift freighter."

"Huh," said John. "Look more like three whores on their backs with their laigs spread."

The Poland Street wharf, as ratty a stretch of pier as there is on the Mississippi, looked like the shore of a promised land. A stretch at sea can make it seem so. Within twenty minutes of securing the last line to the bits, Pooch appeared at the rail decked out in a new turquoise rayon shirt, pressed slacks, and black patent leather shoes. Butts was beside him, unkempt and uncouth, eyes so bloodshot it was a mystery he could see at all, trying to borrow money. Pooch stood firm.

No one could go ashore until customs and immigration had cleared the ship. When the officials arrived, those waiting to board her, including ship agents and chandlers, swarmed up the gangway.

The company paymaster arrived with a beat-up old briefcase containing $150,000 in cash. Payoff was at 10:00 in the officers' mess. The Captain and the mates helped stuff the envelopes. They sat at a table with big stacks of hundred-, fifty-, twenty-, ten-, five-, and one-dollar bills in front of them. Merchant seamen are always paid in cash. They don't trust checks, and most banks wouldn't cash a seaman's checks anyway. The crew lined up in the passageway, and spilled into the mess, happy, shouting. As they were called forward one by one, they seemed suddenly sheepish, and cast down their eyes, or held their caps in front of them with both hands, as though amazed that this cash was actually theirs.

Higgin and Cascabel each drew a little more than $3,600.00, not bad for a month and a half. Almost two-thirds of it was overtime pay, and they'd done a good job of husbanding it, not drawing too much in Bremerhaven. Cascabel was saving his money for college. One more trip on the *Columbianna* and he'd have enough for the first year's tuition. By contrast, Butts got $64.56—all that remained of his wages. He'd taken the rest in advance for booze and poker money. He walked out of the mess declaring he was badly in need of a drink.

After the payoff, the Captain grumbled that the Chief Mate

had made more than he had on account of overtime. The Captain's pay comes to about $45,000 a year; the Chief Mate's to $50,000, because he works extra hours supervising the stowage of cargo in port.

"Hell," said the Captain after a lengthy discourse on the intolerableness of it all, "it ain't that I mind him makin' so much money. It's the *principle* of the thing."

Most of the crew were signing off in New Orleans. Higgin and Cascabel wanted to stay on, but not if the Bosun did. Knowing this, the Bosun announced he was signing on for another trip. He wasn't, but he figured that by waiting till the last minute, he could force the two of them to sign off. They had done him no wrong; why he would want them to leave was—a mystery. He was a perverse old sucker. But Higgin and Cascabel sniffed his bluff. They knew he'd stolen so much gear on board—tools, machine parts, line, paint, chocks, you name it—he couldn't *afford* to stay on. He didn't live far from New Orleans; and it wouldn't be hard to sneak it all past the guards. He'd box it and call it cargo. Still, he'd need a goddam U-Haul to get it home. The waiting game began.

The Yansons, who'd had their gear packed for days, disappeared down the gangplank in a hail of *ya-hooooos.* Slim and Gut waved from the bow, telling them to go easy on their wives. The Yansons had been pretty explicit this last week about what they had in store for "the little women" once they got home after forty days of abstinence. Slim and Gut said they felt sorry for the wives. When the Yansons rounded the corner of the warehouse and were gone, Slim and Gut shook their heads a little, sad to be staying. They both had a lot more money to earn before they could sign off and go home to Norfolk.

Chiefy tended to his calculations. The 5,917-mile trip from Bremerhaven had taken fourteen days, six hours, and twenty-two minutes. A total of 5,443 barrels of Bunker C fuel oil had passed through the nozzles. At $23.50 per barrel, it came to $217,925.00. Six years ago, before the Arab oil embargo, the same fuel bill had been just under $13,500.00. The earliest recorded tramp was owned and skippered by Aurelius Heracles. Aurelius landed a load

213

of vegetable seed in the Mediterranean port of Oxyrhynchus on October 21, 236 A.D. He charged 100 silver drachmas, about $8.00.

The newspapers were full of the Soviet invasion of Afghanistan. Mr. Dexter, cheered by this news, said she would now definitely be going to the Persian Gulf. "She's a hot baby, this one," he said, patting her life rail.

To Mr. Fogarty, the Soviet invasion was also good news, but for a different reason. Every time he saw the Captain he would remark loudly about the certainty of war and the *Columbianna*'s participation in it. The Captain pretended not to hear.

The men who weren't on day shift went ashore, most of them headed toward the French Quarter.

At a pawnshop that boasted a thirty-foot counter of .22-caliber Saturday Night Specials, the Bosun found out the gold bracelets he had "stolen" in Bremerhaven for seven hundred dollars were made of base metal and were worth about twenty-five dollars. A clerk with a diamond pinky ring rubbed them on a whetstone, leaving a suspicious gold-colored smear, then filed a small nick in each of the bracelets and eye-droppered nitric acid into it. The acid turned green; the Bosun turned red. Outside, he said he was going to give them to his wife and tell her they were worth seven hundred dollars anyway. It was the thought that counted. Then he went back to the ship and punched Chiefy in the nose because there was an oil spill outside his focsle.

Before he signed off, Jefferson threatened to kill the insurance claims adjuster. There was no very good reason. He was going home to get his "piece," he said, so he could fix Boykin and Cascabel and the others who had stepped in to break up the fight. But Jefferson did not return to the ship, and was never seen again by any member of the crew.

The Chief Steward returned from a night ashore with stitches over his left eye.

Sparks went on a binge. He came back late, pie-eyed, offering anyone ten dollars to go beat up his cabbie.

Yoya delayed breakfast for half an hour while he preached

on the evils of prostitution to the Baker and Marty. He renewed his expatiations on the hammerhead sharks he said had swallowed Roberto Clemente whole. By day's end the Captain had no choice but to fire him.

He did it for reasons of "crew morale," as he entered it in the dry log. That was true, and an understatement. Word had spread that Yoya was spitting on second helpings when messmen brought plates back to the galley for more. When Higgin heard about this—fortunately after Yoya had gone—he said, "I'd a doggie-wrenched that son of a bitch. He took out the garbage once a day. I'd a waited for him, doggie-wrenched him, and thrown him over the side." He shook his head. "I don't go for that shit."

Sparks appeared in bathrobe and slippers, dreadfully hung over and saying that "goddam sunspots" were interfering with his radio transmissions.

Mr. Fogarty, still cutting keys to fit all the obsolete locks, finally gave up. His leg hurt badly, though he wouldn't admit it. Between that and the keys he couldn't take it anymore. He went to the Captain's office and told him he was going to sign off— that his wife had just had a stroke. The Captain said he was sorry and asked questions about what kind of stroke it was and how was she doing, and Mr. Fogarty said, Well, you know, with these things there is no saying, they could go one way, they could go another. The conversation continued quite some time, the Captain pretending to regret Mr. Fogarty's leaving, Mr. Fogarty pretending his wife had had a stroke, neither fooling the other, until an awkward pause turned into excruciating silence, and Mr. Fogarty said good-bye and left. Outside the Captain's office, he said he was vastly relieved, and that he now realized the Captain was "a secret drinker." The Captain said later, "I tell ya, I think it's *him* had the stroke."

The union sent a new AB to replace one who had left out of hatred for the Bosun. The new man was a young fellow named McGuire, strong, tattooed, an ex-marine paratrooper who had taken part in the rescue of the *Mayaguez*, the U.S. freighter captured by Cambodians just after the fall of Vietnam. Big Mac was standing gangway watch when he came aboard, greeted him, and told the AB his name was McGuire, too.

The new man flinched. "What's your first name?"

"Jim," said Big Mac.

The AB seemed relieved. "Good."

"How's that?"

"You'd said Frank, I'd a killed you."

"Oh," said Big Mac, a little surprised. "How come?"

He said that Frank McGuire was his father, and that he'd never laid eyes on him. "Some day, though—"

Ignacio the oiler came back to the ship saying *puta puta puta*. "What's the matter, Ignacio?"

"I walk into my house," he said, "an' my wife got this other guy there with her in bed. 'Oh man,' she say, 'Why didn' you call?' I say, "Hey, my ship come in soddenly.' She say, "You should call.' I say, 'Oh, man.' An' you know, she hit me up for a fifty—for *him*. He's broke. An' I give her fifty dollars, to give to this guy he's in bed with my wife. Oh man. Well, I ain' finish with that bitch yet."

A .38-caliber slug was found embedded in the spare washing machine on the poop deck. No one standing gangway watch the night before had heard a shot. Chiefy, whose responsibility extended to the washing machines, was incensed, and made unkindly remarks of an ethnic nature about the residents of the neighborhood. He stood there on the poop deck: a small man, angry in the morning sunlight, shaking his fist in the direction of Poland Street, haranguing the invisible enemy.

Yet it seemed appropriate, somehow, that a stray bullet would have come to rest on the deck of an old tramp freighter.

Mail call induced general depression. Nino, Rocco's ex-focslemate, said on the deck afterward; "Man, no one writes me no more." Walking away, he said, "They don't mind it when you send money. Fuck no. Well I don't care anymore."

The home office in New York instructed the Captain to make ready to sail that night for Puerto Rico. They had cut a lucrative deal with the navy. The *Columbianna* was to proceed

216

to the navy base at Roosevelt Roads, pick up a damaged F-14 fighter jet, and deliver it to Norfolk. The sailing board was posted for 2230 hours.

This meant the Bosun had to give up his bluff and hurry to remove his stolen gear before she sailed. The union sent down a new bosun, a big-bellied Cajun on the run from a woman.

Higgin spent the afternoon ashore with some navy chiefs off a destroyer, downing piña coladas and reliving the days when no muff was too tough and no thigh too high. He got back to the *Columbianna* in bad shape, and when the All Hands order came, the new bosun more or less had to drag him out of his bunk all headachy, and spent. As he disappeared into the shower he grumbled that he was "gonna whup ass like ass never been whupped before." He quieted as he towelled dry, and said what was bothering him most was his knee. Two years ago, drunk, doing forty miles an hour on a motorcycle, he'd gone through a guard rail, landing a hundred feet on the other side with his right leg turned completely backward at the knee. He said he had to make up a shopping list for Norfolk. "Knee brace and beer."

Mr. Dexter came back from the port doctor with bad news. He had to sign off. He'd sustained a neck injury months ago when the *Columbianna*'s relief captain slammed her into a Coast Guard cutter in Mobile. It had been giving him a great deal of pain recently. The doctor told him he had to have tests immediately. Mr. Dexter tried to talk him out of it, said to give him some painkillers and he'd get off at the end of the next trip. The doctor said no, and not entirely trusting Mr. Dexter, wrote him up Not Fit for Duty. And that was that. As Mr. Dexter walked down the gangway and left the ship, he said he was planning to stop at the Shrine of Saint Jude on the way to the airport. He looked sad, leaving the "hot baby" he had been sure would take him on his last trip, to the Gulf and beyond and out with a bang.

Not long before she left New Orleans, Butts staggered into the mess. He had spent most of the day passed out in the room with the electrical switches. He drank four cups of coffee, listened to a story about a seaman who used to tape-record his fights with his wife and play them over and over when he was at sea. Apparently it made him feel better about being unfaithful to her. Butts rubbed his eyes, turned, and said "I've never liked the sea. I don't like the sea, and I'll never like the sea. And you know, I'm going to spend my entire life at sea."

In his cabin, changing out of the powder-blue jumpsuit into the vanilla-malt one, the Captain remembered something he'd left out of his story about Typhoon Dinah. He said that after the second day, the sea became glass calm, and they saw the birds, thousands of them, trapped in the eye of the storm.

Epilogue

A few minutes before midnight, the *Columbianna* sailed for Puerto Rico. In the dark, none of the signs of her old age were visible, none of the rust streaks, none of the dings. Her black hull shone under the glare of the spotlights, and there was stubborn dignity in the way she resisted the pull of the tugs. As she moved away from the wharf with a rumbling in her boilers, there was shouting from the bridge. It was the Captain. His walkie-talkie must have failed. He was yelling toward the bow, drowned out by other noises.

As she moved into mid-channel, and the tugs prepared to release their lines, I caught sight of Pooch standing on the poop deck, lighting a cigarette. Pooch saw me there on the shore and waved, and I watched until she rounded a bend down river and was gone.

Acknowledgments

Many people contributed to *Steaming to Bamboola,* not all of them named here. My thanks do not adequately express my debt to them.

HARRY THEODORACOPULOS was kind enough to point me in the right direction at the outset. If the references to Greek sea captains annoy him, my defense is that the information came from his brother TAKI.

ROBERT MOTTLEY was an invaluable ally, and a good friend.

RALPH JASKOW of Hudson Waterways showed me great kindness.

Without MARTY GERSHON, my ship would never have sailed. Without LUCIANNE GOLDBERG, I never would have known the ship was sailing.

AL KANE was my host at Snug Harbor, and a generous friend. My thanks also to Gov. LEO KRASZESKI and his wife PATRICIA for making my stay there a happy one.

CHAPLAIN WILLIAM HAYNESWORTH and CHIEF LIBRARIAN BONNIE GOLIGHTLY of the Seamen's Church Institute of New York were very kind to me.

To RED CAMPBELL of The Seafarers' International Union, and CLYDE BALL of the Maritime Administration, my thanks.

MARVIN LIEBMAN showed me where to begin the long voyage home.

GREG ZORTHIAN and my father and mother read the original manuscript. For that drudgery, and for their suggestions, my thanks.

To MICHIKO KAKUTANI, teacher, friend, editor, she-poet, my poor thanks, and love.

To MELODY LANE, who transcribed the tapes and typed the manuscript, my devotion always.

Without GRETCHEN SALISBURY's shrewd and maddeningly good editing, *Steaming to Bamboola* would have gone up on the rocks.

Without THOMAS CONGDON, whose patience, wisdom, encouragement, and friendship were always with me, there never would have been a book. To him my thanks, admiration, and affection.

For *Steaming to Bamboola*'s many faults no one but I am to blame.

Washington, D.C.
August 25, 1981